EIGHTY-SOMETHING
a lifetime of conversation

Sue Gill & John Fox

Published in 2023 by
Dead Good Guides

© Sue Gill & John Fox

ISBN: 978-0-9568583-4-4

Illustrations by © John Fox

Cover and Book interior design by
www.pixeltweakspublications.com

Cover illustration - linocut 'Hands' by John Fox

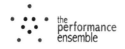

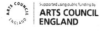

Dedicated to
Bill and Muriel
Dolly and Horace

1001 STORIES is a ground-breaking collaboration for LEEDS 2023 Year of Culture between The Performance Ensemble, Leeds Playhouse, Leeds Museums and Galleries, Leeds Older People's Forum. 1001 STORIES is a celebration of age and ageing, telling stories of lives lived to their fullest from Over 60's resident or working in Leeds. Artistic Director Alan Lyddiard commissioned Sue Gill and John Fox to write a new book for 1001 STORIES Take Over at Leeds Playhouse.

FOREWORD
Alan Lyddiard, Artistic Director,
The Performance Ensemble

The intimate informing the spectacular.

I first met John Fox and Sue Gill, the pioneers of Welfare State International, in 1992 at a seminar/discussion in Ulverston about making work in communities. I had just joined Northern Stage as Artistic Director and I travelled across to join them and others for a weekend of conversation.

It actually opened my mind to possibilites that I had never imagined. They spoke about small moments of connections with people, moments that were seemingly insignificant but that over time were remembered and had become meaningful. Important moments that told us something about ourselves and the world we live in, even though we didn't realise it immediately. They talked about how these people contributed to large artistic events/ statements where hundreds of people came together to create art. A place and time where they connected deeply in a shared experience of creativity. A single connection with one person leading to a collective vision of a community coming together.

This thought stayed with me for many years until in 2020 I met them again when I participated at a week-long workshop 'Rites of Passage' exploring ceremony and ritual that Sue leads regularly with celebrant Gilly Adams. It was at that moment that I knew I wanted to work with them on 1001 Stories - a Take Over of Leeds Playhouse by older people.

Sue and John founded Welfare State International in Leeds, when John became a Senior Lecturer at Leeds Polytechnic. It is therefore totally appropriate that they return to Leeds to co-create the opening event of 1001 Stories. On occasion they work with their son and daughter, Dan (born in Bradford) and Hannah (born in Leeds) - experienced artists in their own right - who joined them to create the opening event with the community of older artists from Leeds and across the world.

This book is a gift to those participants, to older people who came together for a moment to 'make art with the experience of age', reconnecting with people, some of whom have known each other for over 30 years and some who had just met, to make some noise together about the joys of ageing.

CONTENTS

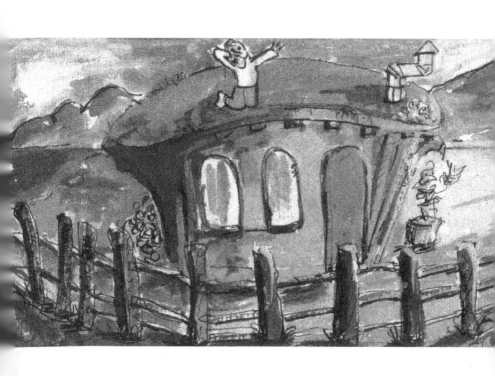

MORNING HOUSE

Wooden stilts anchor the house into the steep slope down to the beach. Walls are built with larch lap, faded silver grey over the years. The turf roof fluoresces pink, yellow and blue in summer with sedum and harebells.

Inside, the living room is lined with bookshelves. Two walls are glass from floor to ceiling, framing the uninterrupted expanse of Morecambe Bay with its huge tidal rise and fall, four times a day. A log burner heats the space. The table expands for gatherings of

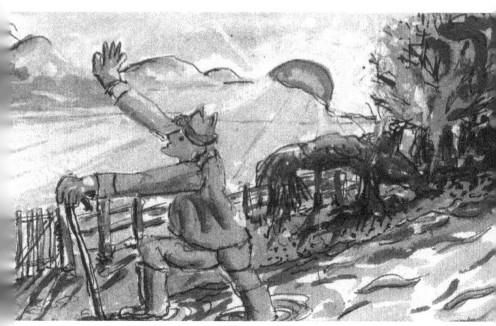

family and friends. There's a cupboard full of musical instruments and another full of dry groceries.

The mezzanine has bedrooms and Sue's writing space.

Robust ash trees emerge through the wooden decks on the east side. This is a place of sunrise, a morning house.

The studio stands a little apart. Custom built, its oval shape contains printing press, deep sinks, etching and woodcut tools, enamelling kiln, drawing and painting resources and two plan chests full of artworks. This is the crucible where ideas, images, books, essays, poetry and projects are born. Between the studio and the house is a stone path and garden, with more decks to catch the afternoon sun.

Visitors heading down to the shoreline pass large poster poems on the wall. Kinetic sculptures come into view - large cut out whirlygigs and weathervanes overhead, each on its tall coppiced pole rotating in the wind. A ghost wolf, a black submarine, a deer leaping away from wildfire … Giant silver cardoon plants thrive and produce a score of purple 'thistles' above our heads.

Tucked into the bank is an adobe style open sided lookout shelter with cobbled floor and seating, built by Duncan Copley and comfortable for four people. Orientated on a North/South axis, it focusses directly across the bay to the Iron Age fort on the summit of Ingleborough forty five km to the East.

The tide retreats and 2000 oystercatchers fly in to feed and rest. The heron keeps his distance, the lonely call of the curlew tells us she is feeding, her long curved beak deep into the seabed. The rooks will have their usual meeting out in the Bay at dusk. This is a place of wind and weather, ceremony and celebration, writing, thinking and dreaming new myths for the future.

After their travels our offspring return, welcomed usually with a feast of salt marsh lamb. Fires on the beach, conversation and music under the stars, grandchildren, neighbours and friends connecting. Occasional ceremonies to welcome a newborn, to mark partnerships, honour significant decades, acknowledge love and loss. After twenty years of living here it is difficult to differentiate between home and workspace, life and art.

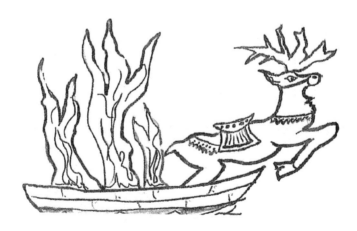

HEART & HANDS

FRAME RAISING 1999

Sue's address to the volunteers:
Duncan, Tommie, Ruud, Ged, Therese,
Dan, Kate, Hannah, Roger and Martin

Building the Beach House represents three commitments for me:

To this place - Cumbria

To John Fox and the long future we will have together here.

To myself.

What is this house to me already? I have not yet slept here, but I sense it is a morning house - sunrise. From early childhood, being at the place where the land meets the sea matters. The Beach House offers stillness, a place to empty out, to quieten down enough to remember who I am.

I have no plans, no projects to undertake. Not for a couple of years anyway. Just to watch the tide come in and out, notice the sky .....

From time to time I hope to be invaded by family and friends, hordes of them, bringing laughter and music, coming to share food and drink - and lots of wine. Neighbours, colleagues. Noise and chaos.

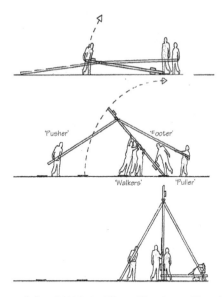

Thank you Chris and Peter, professional builders, for your vision, planning and dedicated work in creating our house on this little plot of land. The Fox Family will cling tenaciously to it and love it, for many years to come.

Today is Wednesday 12th August. In the rest of the UK it is The Glorious Twelfth, to do with hunting and shooting rights. In our tiny kingdom, on our Frame Raising Day, it is simply GLORIOUS.

Thank you all for your help today. Let's drink a toast to Raising the Frames!

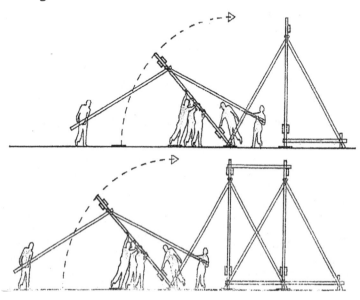

TOUCH

Until I was eighteen I had never seen or touched a piece of clay. After years at a dull High School for Girls, where I had never worked with my hands, never made anything, never been invited to use my imagination, I realised - with hindsight - that any shred of divergent thinking I might have had at eleven years of age must have deteriorated by the time I left.

I am at University training to be a teacher. Creativity is on this syllabus now, offering Contemporary Dance and Ceramics. This is all new to me. Living in Halls on site I have access to the pottery workshop day and night. I fall in love with clay, and the hands-on connection with an elemental material. The sense of touch, moulding, wedging the clay to get the air bubbles out. I stand above the work bench, full body weight forward, down through my hands cupped around a chunk of clay. With thumbs touching, I push through the heels of my hands forward and down, then roll it back towards my body, re-adjust hands as before and start again. Elbows straight, one foot in front of the other. This way it is my back that does the bulk of the work. Thirty to forty times at least. Only then is the clay ready to go onto the wheel to be turned into a pot.

By the end of my course I have no interest in being a teacher and I go off as an unpaid assistant to an eminent studio potter.

Seven years later, on a month's sabbatical from our theatre company, I volunteer at a village bakery on the North Yorkshire moors. I want to learn from the baker how to make bread. At 6.30am I walk down the valley, from our terrace cottage in the middle of a row of miners' houses, to start the dough, before greasing individual bread tins for different sized loaves. Witnessing the dough rise in her warm kitchen, knocking it down for the second rise, then kneading it again on the floured table. Timing is of the essence, watching, understanding temperature, how long to leave it, when to put it in the hot oven and for how long. The test is to take a loaf in its hot tin from the oven, carefully tip it out, turn it over and knock on the bottom. If the loaf sounds hollow it is done, if not, put it back in the tin upside down and into the oven for a little longer, then onto racks to cool.

POSTSCRIPT

Life as a potter can be lonely. Just you and the clay.

As I got less shy and more interested in people and their stories I favoured bread making instead. I developed sculptural figurative loaves for ceremonies and celebrations - all edible and tasty - and taught many others to make and enjoy them.

SANCTUARY

Wearied by Board Meetings and future planning, I took a day out for a recce with a film maker to a Cheese Farm. An organic family business with a small staff in North Cumbria. *A Question of Lunch* was to be the title of our film. It never materialised but spending a day with cheeses has stayed with me.

Their stone building stands in a sunny courtyard. Duck through the low door and close it behind. It's cool inside, and quiet. The cheeses are resting, weathering.

Handmade cheese is a living food and here time takes on a different dimension. No sense of urgency. There must be around two thousand cheeses in rows on wooden racks around the walls, placed three or four deep. Each needs to be turned every day for seven or eight months by careful women who also work in the production unit across the yard. Milk from the cows in the surrounding fields is different every day as the grass changes according to weather and time of year. They work elbow deep in tanks to separate curds and whey, make, mix, shape, press and wrap each cheese separately.

In here it is dry and still. Like a convent, a sanctuary. Patience and obedience. A different centre of gravity. What is it I am I yearning for?

11

Each cheese sits inside her snug muslin wrap, a swaddled garment pulled tight, cloth straining over the shoulders where deft thumbs have pleated and turned it to a good fit. Chalky white on the sides, like old lime wash in a back scullery. A charcoal disc on the top with a mysterious astronomy of mould. Neighbour by neighbour - there's something about unanimity. No resistance, no opinions, just a single focus on the journey of weathering. An innate dignity which commands respect.

To turn a cheese requires two careful hands. As we grasp a hot mug of tea to keep ourselves warm, that is precisely how we must hold a cheese in order to pick it up - surprisingly heavy - turn it and place it back on the rack without touching its neighbour.

If only I could drop everything and come and work here in the weathering shed ……

HEAD, HANDS, HEART
working with our hands

Forty four years ago we moved to South Cumbria where hill farmers, with sheep on remote fells, were traditionally a one family business. Farmers shear the sheep by hand, repair the barn roof, put a wheel back on the trailer, deliver lambs when the ewe gets into difficulties, repair gates and drystone walls … If necessary, a farmer could probably make a coffin and play the accordion at the wake.

In Ulverston local traders run shops and market stalls as a family business. Fruit and veg, small cafes, homemade pie shops, knitting wool, flowers and plants, bakery, newsagent. Of late, forced to close as multi-nationals and drive-thrus are allowed to set up in town.

Away from heritage cobbled streets, a father and son run their own small garage in the former slaughter-house of the cattle market. Skilled motor mechanics. Working with their hands servicing cars, mending bodywork, repairing engines. Making their own decisions, problem solving, drawing on accumulated knowledge and experience. At the end of each working day, face to face with the customer, building trust and relationships, hopefully for a return visit. Hard work, unpredictable, no sick pay or holiday pay, no guaranteed pay cheque - regardless of how much or how little has been achieved - yet proud of their business.

I met a welder working among thousands of employees in a shipyard. He clearly hates his job but is trapped by the usual family responsibilities to bring home a decent regular wage. A good man, he turns up each day.

Busy, alongside scores of others, using his considerable skill to weld one bespoke metal component, again and again, that is needed for the current vessel under construction. Just this one component over and over that he never fits, or sees it in place, fitted by someone who has not made it. Decisions made by staff completely remote from his workbench.

Every day he works conscientiously and on completion of the task, feeling so alienated, he throws the component into the dock. His quiet rebellion, necessary to keep his sanity, his integrity, his self belief. In refusing to contribute to this depersonalised workplace, this is the only path available to him; he has no choice.

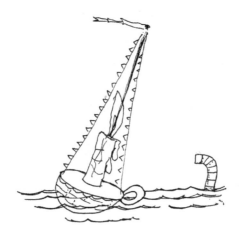

RAG & BONE

LETTER TO MY MUM

Dear Mum,

I've been invited to write a letter about climate and ecological change and send it to anyone I wish. My letter is for you Mum. I know this won't mean much to you. You were born in 1908 and It's nearly forty years since you died, and we weren't talking about such stuff then. I can see you at home Mum, looking after us and the house, diligently day by day. I was 46 when you died. I'm 83 now. Don't feel it. And I've still got a good memory.

Laundry - Monday was washday - you had a deep sink in the kitchen and soap suds from a big bar of soap. You are standing with your arms deep in the sink, scrubbing brush in your right hand. Cuffs and collars - always the grimiest bits. You slap each garment onto the draining board. Scrub, scrub, scrub. Wringing it out with a strong grip - grasping, twisting, squeezing, turning. Thick towels, cotton bedsheets. Rinsing next, then through the hand turned mangle. Hang them out on the line in the garden. Wooden dolly pegs, wooden clothes prop with a V notch in the top to lift the full line up into the wind.

I remember the twin tub Dad bought to make things easier. Wash tub on the left, spin on the right. Filled through a hose from the tap into the wash compartment. Switch it on and it heats up. Lid down, grab the handle on top that moves the paddle below, work it to and fro, thrash clothes, forward and back, round and round. Us kids think this is fun for 5 minutes but you do all the energetic work. Then into the spin drier that flings the water out and back into the sink. Progress.

It feels modern. Next, wash power in a cardboard box and Persil White in our language. You and Nana used a lot of bleach. Poured down sinks indoors and out to keep everything smelling clean. Great God Domestos swilling the yard. We must not do that now; now that we understand what harm it does to creatures in the rivers and in the sea. We use non bio detergents today.

The rag and bone man doesn't come around any more. 'Any Rag Bo-one?' His horse and cart rattling along the back alleys. These days we have to be careful about what we throw away. We can't dump all our rubbish into that old metal bin with the clattering lid, ready for landfill. We must separate cardboard and paper from bottles, from tins, from plastic which gets collected, melted down, made into something else, re-cycled. I know you'd be very tidy with your re-cycling.

So, what happened to low impact off-grid living? What happened to sharing bath water with each other once we showered? I have had an automatic washing machine in the house since the 1980's, but never a tumble dryer. You would be shocked Mum at the electricity they gobble up. The wind outside is free and the clothes smell nice which is a bonus.

We don't, can't, mustn't burn coal anymore. So we've got rid of that smog in towns and bad chests. Electricity warms us from thousands of beautiful wind turbines, often installed row after row in the sea. We see them from miles away. A wind farm? Strange name that. No tractors, no mud, no cattle or crops. Farming the wind!! We farm wave power too - capturing energy from tides and rivers. Scientists and engineers are building life enhancing inventions to look after the land, the air, the oceans.

Young people really get it and are serious about the mess we're in and are calling for governments world wide to wake up urgently and make decisions about how we all might all live safely. We have world wide crises. Storms and floods are coming like we've never seen before. Drought and wild fires too. These are the problems we have to solve, brought on by our own thoughtlessness and greed.

So Mum, what else to say? I've tried hard to keep our children safe and well and, now they are parents themselves, they are doing the same, if not better, for their children. There's a tough future ahead for them which I won't be around to witness. We try to give them resilience and the values of collaboration and community rather than competition and capitalism. I have every faith in their energy and vision. We must think about the dreadful state we are allowing the planet to get into. It's their inheritance, their futures, which is why these letters are important.

With much love and thanks for everything you gave me

Your daughter

Sue Gill x

THINGS THAT STICK
IN THE MIND

1949 Hymers College, Hull. I am 11. Mr Watson, ambitious for his school choir calls us forward one by one testing us to sing the three notes he plays on the piano. I dry. I squawk.

I am rejected and told to mime at the back. 39 years later determined to sing I discover an ex-opera singer living in Ulverston. She has a chequered history related to alcohol, so understands failure, and embarrassment. I go weekly and one day she plays Mr Watson's very three notes. I panic and cry but we have found a threshold and gradually I learn to sing. On occasions I sing in a choir and sometimes with a ukulele ensemble. I am in tune and I love it.

1958 Tamale, Ghana. I am a teenage National Service officer training African soldiers in internal security for President Kwame Nkrumah, who had just declared independence from the Gold Coast (once a centre of the lucrative slave trade). On a routine evening patrol round military quarters I check the latrine to find a foetus on the ground. I am not sure what it is but the resident Medical Officer helps and says it isn't unusual. *"They are usually buried by The Medical Centre. No need for a coffin."* After a while I remember ammunition boxes. So we use them in the future. The MO told us much later that they were now getting their best ever crop of geraniums.

1968 Instow, North Devon. Sue Gill is 6 months pregnant with Dan, our son, who is now 54 and a successful professional musician. Taking an evening off rehearsing an event, we sit in the front row of the Lobster Pot – a bar and music venue. Mike Westbrook's wild concert band is playing *Release*. Framed by a massive setting sun in the window behind them, the band drives formidably loud jazz, Dan leaps high, kicking inside Sue's belly. Born on 27th November he has played trombone and taught percussion ever since.

2021 Beach House, Cumbria. On the jetty over looking the coastal path. I squidge strips of glued cloth round clumps of sea washed wood. I am creating a nasty black dog. Crouched, ready to pounce with an open jaw, lobster claw teeth, rubber glove tongue and yellow glass eyes. Black Dog waits, checking out hikers and dog walkers. Their pets back off. Black Dog is an externalisation of despair. A manifestation of depression. A symbol to acknowledge and deal with a common condition. Winston Churchill used the same metaphor. So did Paul Nash the artist. It's in my glossary of archetypes too. Putting your mind in your fingers does help.

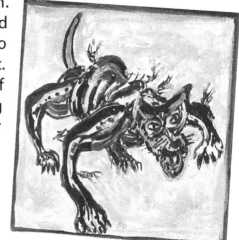

FIRST TIME

First home - evacuated, wooden cabin in a field, Mum, my Auntie and me away from bombs.

First bowl - for porridge, heavy flat bowl, hares run round the rim, put it outside to cool.

First pram - sitting up, my finger tip feels smooth buttons holding lining round the edge.

First garden - flowers tall as my face as I toddle through, aroma of blackcurrant bushes.

First song - *Mairzy Dotes and Dozy Dotes and Liddle Lamzy Divey* - a novelty song from 1943 sung in the dark shelters during air raids so children don't cry.

First clothes - cotton dress with short puffed sleeves, elastic too tight on my plump arms.

First dance school - age 3, shuffling to copy big girls in tap shoes. *You are my Sunshine.*

First bike ride - back of Mum's bike downhill, summer sandals, bare toes stuck in the spokes.

First meals - sandwiches, hating bread, sneak out to the garden, throw them to the birds.

First cafe - glass top tables, ladies' gossip, cakes, my bare thighs on scratchy cane seats.

First day at school - resting on tiny camp beds, looking up into Miss Bowen's brown eyes.

First book - Hedgehog story for my birthday, finished it on the first afternoon. What now?

First foraging - collecting bronze coloured seeds by the handful, sliding them up off the tall stems of the Dock plant into my tin, shut the lid, keep to sprinkle as fairy dust.

First wireless programme - Dick Barton Special Agent. Don't miss next week's episode!

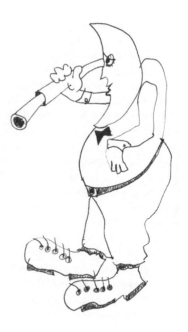

First cinema - Wizard of Oz. Cackling broomstick. Witch flies off with Dorothy's dog.

First responsibility - age 11, take younger brother weekly on the bus to tiled Physio clinic torture.

First drudgery - age 14, head wind both ways cycling to High School on heavy Hercules.

First scooter - age 23, Lambretta, gear changes stall up steep North Yorkshire hills, impossible to hold the weight, to restart. No-one around. Tears.

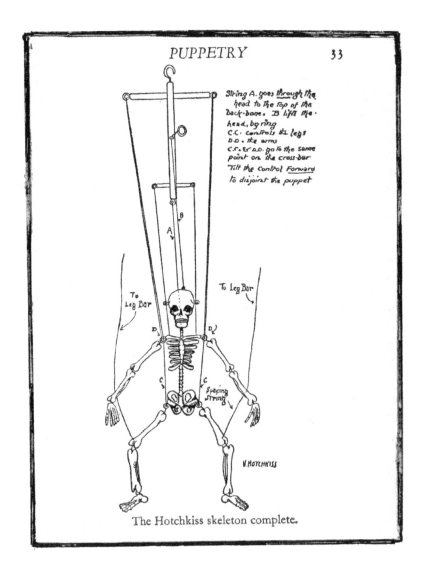

String A. goes through the head to the top of the back-bone. B lift the head, by ring
C.C. controls the legs
D.D. the arms
C.C. & D.D. go to the same point on the cross-bar
Tilt the control Forward to disjoint the puppet

To Leg Bar

To Leg Bar

Spacing String

V. HOTCHKISS

The Hotchkiss skeleton complete.

SKELETON

I scrounged a large framed poster from John Macfarlane, the international opera designer. His painting for Mozart's Don Giovanni depicts a huge skeleton drawn in white yet entangled in bloody tendrils, clutching and clawing a tiny mortal, reduced to a soggy cig paper or a used condom. It is too scary to display inside. I left it in the garage where the glass shattered. Now it is too scary to dismantle.

Skeletons have always grabbed me. When I was ten I made a marionette skelly fifteen inches tall. Carved from balsa wood with a very sharp knife, it was cunningly engineered, courtesy of *Specialised Puppetry* by H.W.Whanslaw and Hotchkiss 1948. As you tip the hand held controls forward the strings slacken to release jointed bones into a jolly dance of death.

In his macabre graphic *Dance of Death* Hans Holbein the younger (1497-1543) created one of the most brilliant and grisly art works of the Renaissance. In 51 separate hand engraved wood blocks each 65x 48 mm (four small postage stamps in a rectangle) he depicts different vigorous and terrifying skeletons grabbing and hustling the rich, the vain, the poor, the unassuming and the unaware. The graphic skill is outstanding. The message unassailable. Today Death is not expressed so graphically, so bluntly or so clearly.

 Maybe that's a loss. Count the ribs. We all have 12 pairs that's 24 in all.

MUTTON BIRDS

In 1979 after a six month working tour of Australia we put down a deposit on a classic tin roofed bungalow in Stanley, a hamlet on the north coast of Tasmania. We were exhausted. A place to stop. To emigrate and rear children in dynamic sunshine. Stanley was exotic. Bill Mollinson's Permaculture was based there - we discovered. Light aircraft landed on the beach and mutton birds lived in burrows on the hill. A delicacy. Put your hand down. If warm, a chick was there. If cold it had been eaten by a poisonous carpet snake, still waiting. Mutton birds were off our agenda but growing food and art in partnership with Bill M. was alluring. So were bush dances.

But no. My father age 77 in Scarborough had a heart condition. I was his only relative and it would have been cruel to abandon him. The Gods had the dice upside down. We lost our deposit, the owners bought a yacht and we moved into a Georgian terrace house in Ulverston, Cumbria (the birthplace of Stan Laurel) where the back of our property opened on to Stanley Street.

I bought a melodeon and forty years later Fox Family Band is playing for our annual Barn Dance booking for Windermere Sailing Club. Sue is calling, Hannah plays fiddle, Dan, on trombone, is the father of our twin grandchildren Luca and Bel. They are eight, similar ages to Dan and Hannah when in Tasmania. Luca our percussionist maintains steady danceable rhythm, while Bel (when she is not demonstrating steps with Sue) takes Dan's camera phone, leaps on a chair, videos for ten steady minutes, uploads her documentary to Facebook and achieves 300 hits before her bed time.

Maybe the Gods were right after all?

HANDFULS OF CLAY

A clay figure three inches high lies on his back in a slatted wooden box on the windowsill by my desk. Stocky legs and toes, no neck, one arm above his head as if he was doing the Sailors' Hornpipe. Left hand broken off, now lies on his belly. Eyes open, so is his mouth. Not exactly a smile - could be a howl. It was a gift handmade and fired, unglazed, by Peter Bruce Dick a lifelong friend and potter. Peter's life and Jill's, his partner were inextricably linked by coincidence to ours. Yet it was some while before this came to light.

I qualified as a teacher but before I took up a job, I headed South West to volunteer for a few months in a couple of studio potteries. At college I had fallen in love with clay, not education, not children, just clay. Me and the clay.

At a special event at Winchcome Pottery, Ladi Kwali, a renowned potter from Northern Nigeria, demonstrated her skill. She worked in the centre of an open stretch of grass, as we stood around - artists, staff from the pottery, gallery owners, critics, other potters … Using just her hands and coil upon coil of raw moist clay, she created one tall, symmetrical pot from the ground up. Effortlessly the dark red pot grew to Ali Baba proportions in no time. She never spoke. I knew no-one there; my attention was fully on her technique.

A coach pulls up from Gloucester and scores of art students, including Jill, join us. My memory of that day I put in a drawer. It stayed there for a few years undisturbed.

John was not long back from two years' National Service in Ghana. After a misdirected start doing an academic degree, he remedied that by studying Fine Art at University of Newcastle upon Tyne. No grant. I offered to be the bread winner and took a teaching post in the North Yorkshire moors as Head of one of the smallest village schools in England. Eight pupils between five and eleven years - children of hill farmers. I lived in the school house - a lonely, isolating life.

Having read in the local press about a certain Peter and Jill who had bought disused barns and an orchard with a view to opening their own pottery nearby, we drove down the valley one weekend and knocked on their door. Soulmates maybe? A couple of hours later, around their kitchen table, Peter opened a narrow drawer and produced a bunch of tiny photographs of the Winchcombe event. Whilst pretending to photograph the star, he had been taking photographs of me. Then the coach drew up and his dilemma began. Who should he chat up? The rest is history.

Conversation continued. National Service came up. Peter had been sent on the same posting as John, but a year before. The pattern was to move them from base to base every three months. Peter's last base was Tamale in the north. That was John's first.

John moved into the round house that Peter had just vacated.

Their surprise twins were born. We had moved to Bradford for work, our children came along a bit later, but we kept in touch and did Naming Ceremonies together.

Over forty years Jill and Peter produced award winning English Slipware - useful pots with a distinctive glaze achieved by wood ash falling inside the huge kiln he built. We assembled a treasured collection of bowls, and plates which are still in use. It was fortunate he and Jill got together, shaping their lives, feet firmly earthed. I would never have had the perseverance to keep going with that single focus as Jill did.

We did not realise just how ill Peter was. Cumbria to Coxwold, their village, was not an easy journey. All the while at the Beach House, plates we'd used daily since the 1980's began to break for no apparent reason.

After years of increasing dialysis Peter died at home. He requested his ashes be put in the earth under the churchyard wall where the gardener tips the prunings.

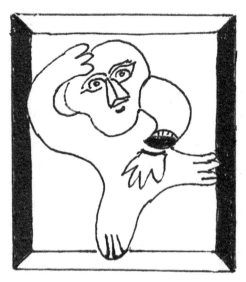

Every time I open the window blinds by my desk I catch sight of Peter still waving.

MBE

In 1977 Ken Loach socialist and brilliant film director (Age 86 in 2022) turned down an OBE. *"One of Betty's gongs. It's not a club you want to join when you look at the villains who've got it. It is all the things I think are despicable: patronage, deferring to the monarchy and the name of the British Empire, which is a monument of exploitation and conquest."* In 2023 Alan Cumming, actor and US Traitors Reality TV host, handed back his OBE over toxicity of Empire. In 2012 John Fox was awarded an MBE for: "Unstinting contribution as an inventor of forms of creative participation and celebration. As a leading exponent of celebratory arts in the UK you have inspired and trained hundreds of community leaders across the UK." I accepted it.

I declined Buckingham Palace and chose instead Ulverston Town Hall for a small ceremony witnessed by 20 friends and family. The Lord Lieutenant, Claire Hensman, pinned the medal onto my lapel. I produced a hacksaw suggesting I should saw it in half as 50% of my achievement was due to Sue Gill. Panic and joke over, I recalled my Merchant Navy father Capt. H. H. Fox MBE, decorated for surviving huge dangers with his skilled command of convoys of ships in the North

Sea in World War 2. I wondered what he would have thought, comparing the merits and differences of father and son gongs. I was surprised but unashamedly delighted to share such accolades with my Dad. We never really had much in common.

Yet a (fairly) well meaning artist colleague messages me with the Ken Loach rejection speech. Wagging a finger. Yet... during the Queen's Funeral I wagged my own finger. Such expense, vanity, power and hypocrisy, fed and maintained by imperialist empire, autocracy, fake democracy and class. I am glad that my granny didn't have to go to her grave on a gun carriage.

So what about the MBE?

In 2011 the Duke of Lancaster's regiment was given the Freedom of Ulverston and 160 soldiers marched through the town with fixed bayonets. The regiment had a sullied reputation. Corporal Donald Payne - amalgamated into the regiment after its formation -became Britain's first convicted war criminal after pleading guilty with other company members to abusing Iraqi detainees, including involvement in the death of Baha Mousa in 2003. As an ex army officer (!) with colonial experience (!) I wrote formally to the Town Council to suggest it was inappropriate to welcome this particular regiment and their bayonets into a town seeking to trade on good will and celebration (with knife crime nationally on the rise).

My letter had no effect. If I'd had my gong at the time I wonder if my intervention would have had more clout?

Maybe it did later when I wrote to our Tory MP to ask him to intervene for an asylum seeker from The Gambia who eventually did gain citizenship. Finger waggings - even self imposed ones - can be unnerving. But so is relinquishing any lever of power that may come by chance. One that can maybe, on occasion, facilitate necessary change. A conundrum of belonging, or just the kettle calling the pot black or even white?

MBE. More Bloody Embarrassment!

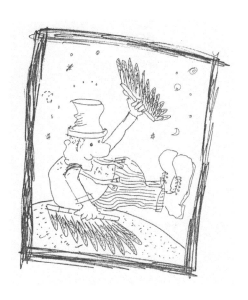

FLESH & BLOOD

CANCER

On the 30th November 2020 I had surgery for rectal cancer and after brilliant attention over nine nights in Furness General hospital I was back home. Then in January 2021, following a routine check up, I was diagnosed with Covid 19 and had to remain in hospital for a further six nights. Both hospital occasions were profound experiences. I was overwhelmed with the skill and care of both staff and patients and wrote about it in *The Rain Days*, a small book of poems which helped my recovery and acknowledged our amazing NHS.

The classic wake-up call. But for skilled diagnosis, rapid treatment and a dedicated wife and family, I could be dead. Essentially Dr Frazer, Miss Patel - *The best scalpel this side of the Pennines* - and Sue Gill saved my life.

I hope it is not indulgent or morbid to focus here on my medical details. I believe they demonstrate rational thinking, logic, necessary pragmatism and hope. And just how lucky we all are, especially me.

Here's part of an email (December 2020) I sent to Tim Fleming who had himself been undergoing treatment for melanoma cancer, for over a decade.

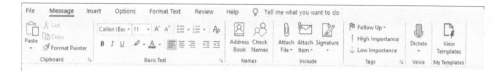

Hi Tim,

Thank you very much for your continuing concerns. Miss Patel assures me they have cut out all the cancer ie 3 centimetre tumour and 27 lymph glands (4 of which were cancerous) from the back passage. Several centimetres of tubing gone to be reversed in six months time. May need a little preventative chemo to be decided later. Stoma bag an unusual companion, but fitting in to appropriate and speedy routine despite tuneful farting at less appropriate moments. Usually reasonably well behaved though.

At home:

One daily injection to thin the blood.

One daily yellow pill to make the willie wee.

Four daily small tumblers of red syrup to thicken the poo.

One morning Ramipril for blood pressure.

One evening Simvustatin for cholesterol.

And a bourbon biscuit for luck.

So here we are. Welcomed home by an incredibly supportive family, especially Sue. They have researched furniture, bathroom require-ments, diet and bought a special bed and mattress. The bed, now downstairs next to the bathroom, has an ejection system which throws me to the piano in two seconds. So Tim, I am learning to play our compositions. All good. So good to be alive. Sleeping well and a lot of it.

Do hope we see you soon.

All our love. John

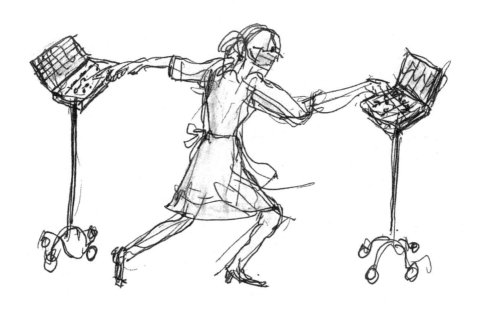

POSTSCRIPT 1: Tragically Tim died, age 63 in January 2022. (*See An Invocation for Tim page 69*)

During his last year Tim worked ceaselessly and generously on *Foxy's Song Book* for which he was a major composer. Given the dreadful pressures of his last year (ending with hospice treatment at home) his dedication to my song words and his own beautiful CD *By Your Side* (available on Bandcamp) was remarkable.

POSTSCRIPT 2: As promised by Miss Patel, the plumbing in my back passage was successfully reversed mid 2021. Goodbye Stoma bags and cancer. Amazing!

BONE DEEP

In my four score years I have had my share of those universal experiences: losses, challenges, adventures, and sometimes failures, and been lucky to be recognised for my work. But there was one rite of passage still to come that required me to be stripped of personal possessions and to submit myself with total trust into the hands of others. There would be no going back. A journey through unfamiliar territory, entering a tunnel of medical mysteries. The mighty NHS, which I see as a river, has been flowing beside me all this time. Only once or twice in eighty years have I needed to dip in a toe, until now, until complete immersion. I need to have my crumbling painful right shoulder replaced.

Mr Monga, NHS Orthopaedic Surgeon, designed and customised an implant, a once-off 'back to front' device made in Italy from titanium by the engineers at Lamborghini. It cost £10K to make, and was fitted by Mr Monga and his team at Wrightington Hospital, centre of excellence for the correction of deformities in bones and muscles.

Is it the middle of the night? All the lights are low or off in this hospital ward. A nurse in quiet shoes slides open the curtains around my bed, mouthing silently that she will take my blood pressure, pulse and temperature.

She points out the Nurse Call Button and the morphine driver to deliver a shot straight into a vein every ten minutes and leaves.

I discover the wound dressing on my right upper arm and shoulder. I have never seen anything so thick. A strange custard colour, yet it feels like a strip of truck tyre with a tread so thick it could function off-road.

Left handed, I furtle with the zip on my bag, take out a pen and spiral bound Reporter's Notebook perfect for a one handed writer. There is no way I can go to sleep. Too much to take in. I need to record this unfamiliar medical world before I forget. A hand comes through the curtain. Plonks a plate and cutlery on my table.

"Pie and Mash."

"Pardon."

"Pie and Mash," and she's gone.

I may not have eaten for 24 hours. Thanks, but - no thanks, not just now.

Like the last person awake on an expedition I sit up with a tiny light writing up the day's fieldwork, as others sleep around me. My world has just gone very small.

I can't get out of bed. Three lines are inserted into the back of my left hand - antibiotics, morphine and fluid for my kidneys. Oxygen comes up to a tiny 'handlebar' clip into each nostril. On my right, blood is draining from the wound into a heavy bag. The blood is a disturbing yellowish colour because it is visible only through this thick plastic tube. I am strapped up tight in a black sling held in place against my bare skin by three straps of military grade Velcro - so tough I reckon I could be winched up into the air.

5.10 am. No sleep. Pie and Mash gone cold. I am in Discharge Ward A, Bay 02, Bed 11. Four women in this bay, our beds arranged around the room, feet pointing towards the centre. I am the last to come in and the oldest. The woman opposite me is quite large. She did not move a muscle all night. White sheet stretched smooth over her domed belly and plump thighs, arms tucked obediently inside, chin peeping at the top. A sing-a-song-of-sixpence white enamel pie dish ready to be baked.

My bed is an island. Gulliver like, I am tethered fast. Porridge for breakfast poured creamy from a thermos jug. Toast and marmalade spread for me, still wearing the hospital gown which can't come off while this sling is in place. In the mirror I am shocked to see slashes of deep yellow iodine around the shoulder area, sloshed on I guess to disinfect.

Back at home and one week later I look back on the the mystical, the everyday and the once-in-a-lifetime experience. A daily bowl of prunes —tinker, tailor, soldier, sailor— will help to rebalance the effect of pain relief drugs, anaesthetics, blood thinners, and sundry unfamiliar substances still in my body. During this liminal journey —still ongoing— I have met strangers, received gifts through kindness, and shared laughter. Nothing will be the same again. It is in there, part of me, and as long as I avoid strong magnets it should be plain sailing.

"When the time comes," my brother remarked, impressed by the value, *"we won't bury you, we'll weigh you in at the scrap yard."*

I am squeamish at the thought of the dressing soon to be removed. By chance the Nurse peels off the dressing without me even noticing. Delighted with the healing, she is confident no further dressings are needed. Hallelujah!!

My daily seated exercise is to journey in a metaphorical rocking boat. Right arm now free from the sling for a few minutes, I lower it over the starboard side, stretch in deep to scoop up a handful of water in my palm and bring it up to 'bathe' the wound on my shoulder. Repeat, repeat. Then I grasp the tiller, elbow tucked in, and move it steadily outwards and back. I study the tides and currents. Time to put the sling back on.

Four years later. All good, no pain, no problems. Back to pruning bushes, cycling, stacking logs, trundling my wheelbarrow … A new woman, transformed.

HOSPITAL VOCABULARY

I'm in a car park on top of the Pennines in March, freezing cold. The last one to be leaving the meeting, late afternoon. As I struggle to open the car door, the gale knocks me flat on the floor and I break my wrist. No choice.

I find a way to hook the injured wrist over the centre of the steering wheel and drive home forty miles along the motorway, very slowly, using just my left hand. Hymns from my High School Assembly sixty years ago surge forward from the back of my brain. I sing at the top of my voice which keeps me breathing. Car windows wide open.

She who would Valiant be 'gainst all disaster! Let her with constancy follow the M6 … Thanks John Bunyan 1688.

A rare visit to hospital for a purple resin cast to be put over the break.

I am noticing a new vocabulary in my head. Accident, body blow, injury, endurance. To endure is to experience pain, hardship, difficulties and to bear it patiently. Ah! The patient. The person receiving treatment by a doctor. It comes from the Latin patiens meaning suffering.

We have incorporated some visceral turns of phrase into our everyday speech: black eye, thick ear, lick those wounds, rub salt into the wound, that sticks in my throat, breaks my heart, she's a pain in the neck, thorn in my flesh, gets in my hair, under my skin, we're flesh and blood ….

But what about those strong bones in our limbs - Radius & Ulna? Tibia & Fibula?

New Shakespearean names for young couples frolicking before they come a cropper.

The wrist healed fine on its own, no need for treatment. Back to driving.

SEA WASHED GLASS

ONE TIME ROCK

About a quarter of a mile North East of the Beach House, in our bit of Morecambe Bay, there lies a substantial limestone rock, a waymarker and a family talisman. When our children were little they climbed on it, grazing their legs. It has always been there. Now when the tides are right, the winds low and my knees are up to it, we venture out to pay homage.

Certainly the best spot to scatter my cremated remains. Distance, solitude, calmness - a simple sprinkling of ashes into the gentle salt water round our ancient friend. From where, as a ghost at my wake, I will see, on the beach, braziers sparking and a white marquee, illuminated with laughter, whisky driven songs and barbecued chicken.

But things change. January 2023 the horizon is suddenly uneven. Rock's place is distorted. Some beast has clawed the sand to ravage out sixty big boulders to reveal the detritus of civilisation. Car battery, axle, rusted iron girders and a blue plastic jerry can, stuck and full of suspect gunk. All too heavy to lift. Not sure any more if this the place to be laid to rest. The ashes of my sea captain father were scattered at the mouth of the Humber Estuary off the North Sea. I would like something similar.

THE ROCK

In *The Peace of Wild Things* poet Wendell Berry says:

'When despair for the world grows in me and I wake ….
in fear of what my life and my children's lives may be'.…
then, he tells us, he goes out and lies down by the edge of the lake.

'I come into the presence of still water.
And I feel above me the day-blind stars
waiting with their light. For a time
I rest in the grace of the world' ….

For me it's not a lakeside. I walk out at low tide half a kilometre over the seabed to The Rock. A single limestone rock carried here by a glacier slowly travelling south ten thousand years ago and dumped at this spot as it melted. It is always there, visible from the house, except on high tides which cover it for a few hours. Always subtly changing, according to the pool that surrounds it, reflections, clouds, the weather and the ribbing of tiny shells and seaweed.

The Rock is a significant lonely place out in the empty Bay, somewhere for me to reflect, to gain a perspective on what is happening. A place that is integral to my lifetime journey, and my connection to that place is a secure vantage point, useful in unsettling times. Looking back from the Rock, the Beach House is scarcely visible among the ash trees.

We do like to be beside the seaside. It restores us.

SEA WASHED GLASS

A trace of sand left in my jacket pocket is a good sign. Evidence that on my last beach walk I must have brought home some sea washed glass. A couple of pieces on a good day. Thumbnail size. Green glass usually, sometimes blue, occasionally amber and frequently milky white. Smooth, rounded edges from tumbling through the ocean. Easier to spot after rain as the colours deepen when wet.

I've collected sea washed glass for years. Every piece must have its own story. Did it start off as a beer bottle dropped on a Caribbean coast? Or a wine bottle fallen overboard from a boat way out in the ocean?

I give it as gifts, regarding it as a sort of talisman [or talis-woman] for friends to take away after their visit. For a sick neighbour who loved her beach walks, I took a square glass pot, half filled it with the pieces, added water, then placed it on a windowsill so she could see its translucence from her bed.

In his poem *Happiness is the Art of being Broken*, Australian poet Bruce Dawe sees similarities between old people - ground smooth by circumstance - and sea washed glass. He writes with warmth and sadness about ageing and approaching death - all identity lost - yet ends the poem with children roaming beaches, picking up green glass, holding it up to the light and seeing the same transformed world that we knew.

WAVE FROM THE OCEAN

We didn't come into this world. We came out of it, like a wave from the ocean. Alan Watts

In his book *The Sea* written sixty years ago, John F Kennedy asks why is it that all of us are so committed to the sea? He suggests it is because all of us have in our veins the exact same percentage of salt in our blood as exists in the ocean.

It is true that we have salt in our blood, in our sweat, in our tears. From this JFK maintains that we are tied to the ocean and therefore when we go back to the sea we are going back from whence we came.

OLD STORIES

BELLWOMAN

My favourite story of all time is about the bellwoman[*]. I read it over and over - preferably out loud to myself - not just for the narrative but for the form it is held in.

There are sixteen short paragraphs. Each begins *I am* … ends on an elemental word: *bones, night storm, the dead, sea god* … which gets repeated and folded into the start of the next paragraph.

Set in ancient time along a coastline, cliffs collapsing and ravaged by storms. No lighthouses. Sailors and fishermen out in the darkness in their boats. Whenever she senses storm or fog, the white-haired bellwoman makes her way to the church through the tilting graveyard. She climbs the steps to the belfry - 'saucer steps' worn over generations - to heave the two ton bell on its rope until her hands are raw and bleeding.

The exhausted boat out at sea groans, creaks, weeps salt tears as the furious snarl of the sea god taunts the fishermen towards the rocks and quicksands.

"I am the Night Storm and there will be NO morning."

"I am the morning," comes a new voice, greeting the crew with light, calm and safety.

"I am good morning. Let me give you back your eyes."

---

* To be found as *Sea Tongue* in *The Old Stories* by Kevin Crossley-Holland Dolphin Paperback

The fishermen insist there has never been a belfry along this coast for centuries, yet last night they did hear the bell sounding from the bed of the sea, its tongue green and gold, cast in bronze.

ONE FOR SORROW
an OLD STORY from the Howgill Hills in Cumbria

I AM THE DEATH CROW. I see it all. I witness every death in the valley.

Years of farming stony ground on the eastern flank and Arthur Tyson, widower, is harsh as nails. His two sons Seth and Finn, bound by duty, must tread his grinding trail. They shepherd lost dreams of young brides they may never find.

I AM THE DEATH CROW. I sense the hammer and weapon of war in the air.

I AM THE GREAT WAR. My rumours rumble the valley. Adventure and glory. Defy me if you dare. Seth grabs the moment and vanishes like a speck in the distance.

I AM THE DEATH CROW. I know about patience and time.

I AM THE TELEGRAM the father dreads.

Arthur Tyson sets to work, hacking into rocky ground, digging deeper and deeper into despair. His shovel heavy laden. With oak and ash, hawthorn and elder, holly, juniper and a scattering of birch, he will bring to life a wood in the shape of a heart. This heart, his heart that he never knew he had. Work is his way of coping.

I AM THE DEATH CROW. I hear no prayer - only fury and a father howling.

He piles stone on stone, bleeds his hands from foundations to footings, from throughs to coping stones. This drystone wall, battered to slope off winter's rain, to frame his loss. A fortress to keep everyone out. Out for ever.

I AM THE DEATH CROW. I watch the wood grow, lift its branches tall. A perfect green heart on the hill. Oak and ash, hawthorn and elder, holly, juniper and a scattering of birch. In a fork of the mountain ash I build my nest, from bleached rib bones of sheep, scattered on the fell. I watch and wait, but not for long.

Soon, news of World War Two creeps over the land and Finn is gone, to die for others' vanity and foolishness.

I AM THE SECOND TELEGRAM shaking like an aspen leaf.

I AM THE DEATH CROW. I understand turmoil.

Arthur Tyson takes his axe to slash his sorrow through the wood. Through oak and ash, through hawthorn and elder, through holly, juniper and a scattering of birch. Top to bottom, side to side. Sturm und drang. Unquenchable grief, blundering blindly and alone. His life's work over.

I AM THE DEATH CROW. I fly into the valley of death that no-one visits. No children. No grandchildren.

Travellers come from the north, from the south, drawn by the power of legend. They stare over to the east to see with their own eyes a broken hearted wood.

MR PUNCH

It should be easy to write enthusiastically about Punch and Judy and to start with it is.

It's 1948. I am 10. I am centred and happy, conjuring up a papier mache glove puppet head. Over many moons I have desired that mood again. The trappings are simple. On my own, cosy in my mother's kitchen, warm with an AGA, I am working on a big oak table protected with newspapers. My hands are squashing soaking wet shredded newsprint, mixed with flour glue, round a cardboard tube. Into the oven it goes, smelling vile. Then an undercoat, detailed painting, crepe hair, costuming and... Hey Presto here is Mr Punch!

Why Punch? Well, of course he used to be on every beach. Always was. I have seen countless versions of this monster, psychopathic wife beater, baby murderer, sadistic racist and jolly clown entertaining the children. So naturally as a 10 year old apprentice puppeteer I copy the received model from the dominant culture. Punch is embedded in our beings, as unquestioned as John Wayne is to the gun lobby in America.

Universal: timeless and long standing, he is in a Hogarth painting of 1754. Roots are in Commedia dell'Arte, Turkey's shadow puppet Karagoz, Grand-Guignol in Paris, English street theatre and maybe even prehistoric fertility rituals!

As an archetype, Punch attracts different auras. A cruel and wicked maniac (Putin), an egocentric bully (Boris Johnson), a comic anarchic wrecker (Frank Randle, Groucho Marx, Tommy Cooper). A fantasist who wields his Big Stick to demolish anything in his way. An ugly hunchback (Quasimodo) with a hooked nose, squeaky voice, and spindly legs. A cripple to be laughed at (in the old days). An icon to be pitied, admired or feared. As a jester with tomfool colours, clever puns and jokes he makes us laugh at ourselves. He literally beats or cunningly tricks those violators of our freedom: policemen, doctors, hangmen, ghosts, devils, shrews and bawling babies! Is Punch's Tale a useful satirical burlesque in which he mocks morality, marriage, paternity, friendship, learning, law, order, death and the devil himself to show us that life is just an empty joke?

But how is a boy of 10 to know all this? Then and now we are programmed and colonised by our history, cultural templates and habits, global news outlets and social media. But outcomes can be changed! Even within traditional Punch and Judy shows different endings have evolved. I like the one when Punch, in partnership with Clown Joey, folds up the policeman, jams him into a coffin as both dance off singing *"Here we go round The Mulberry Bush."*

Another surprise ending is when the Crocodile appears from outside the booth to drag Punch down (to Hell?). This reveals, I argue, that from an ecological perspective the one thing Punch can't control is the power of Nature. So, taking my cue from a fantasist Punch and inspired by an 11,000 year old skeletal Elk in the Harris Museum in Preston, I re-invent this Elk as '*The*

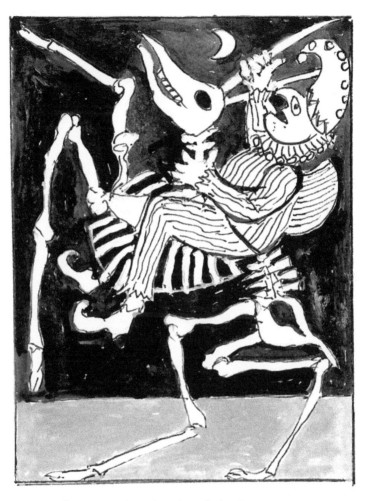

Keeper of Ancient Wisdom' and design a poster poem depicting a pinstriped politician Punch grappling with and failing to strangle the same mythical elk. In my poster Punch has the persona of a controlling maniac trying to exterminate Truth. Just as our 'original' Mr Punch needed to 'Big Stick' his own terrifying ghost. The horror being, in fact, his own conscience, which, of course, knows the Truth. Tell that to Mr Putin and to Mr Blair too!

ALONE

ALONE

For Graham Mansfield (73) marking the
courage of his tragic suicide pact with and
for his wife Dyanne (71) on 23 March 2021.

The sand is hard. Takes a walking stick.
Way out in the lonescape of the Bay,
this Rock is our talisman.
Here we polish moments and scatter ashes.
Soon our wedding anniversary, the diamond one.
You two, forty years shared before the cancer.

I need to be alone on Rock.
Not your aloneness though.
I read you were a baggage handler,
channeling sunny dreams of holiday palavers.
What really holds life together?
I scribble a couple of thoughts.

Suddenly off the sands an old man with his grandson.
"Are you writing a story?"
Yes a poem about a tragedy and a very brave man.
Turns out my visitor was a care worker:
"I know they often up the morphine.
Not shortening life but shortening death."

His grandson is playful. T shirt spells FEARLESS.
Leaping over Rock and its tidal pool,
now black as blood in the fading light,
the boy runs off for a moment to the rising tide.
"Can't do that with a triple by-pass!"
smiles Grandad as they trek back home.

A chance gust grabs my notes.
Sodden, silted and gone.
Below the surface a tiny fish
glints silver in the go-away sun.
Probably a sea bass;
they do breed in the Bay.

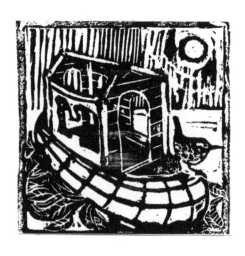

AN INVOCATION FOR TIM

The hills are shrouded in a malignant sadness.

Death is real.
Death is complete.
Death tells us there is no going back.
We can clutter the moment with melodrama,
with ghost train skeletons.
We can wrap ourselves in the
strangle hold of winding sheets bound too tight.
And weep. And weep. And we must.
We will of course linger on body dust fragmenting
to eternity.
But the reality of death is loss.
Where is my husband?
My dad? My grandad?
My brother? My child?
Where is my friend to laugh with over cheese pie
and gossip, over too much wine and chords dimin-
ished.
We recap and regroup.
Search for some genetic switchback of evolution.
Listen to voices in the pleats of the accordion on the
shelf.
They speak of wonder. Memories glow with song.

ONCE

One time there was no time.
Before history got hold of us and we could date
the nails in the cross,
we loved the cycle from seeds to blossom to fruit
and ate apples with no worries.
When Winter came we hoped and knew
that as the moon waxed and waned balefully
under the fixed eye of the sun,
the beacon would flame again.
We knew our bones held the pattern of mud fish.
That calcium was part of the earth and the stars
and always had been
and always will be.
So when our teeth chatter in cold fear
the rhythm echoes in Banyan trees
in acorn cups and bowls
in urns and earth.
The song we strike is the song of Eternity,
which in the spring of creation rises still;
spouting a flood of love
which remains. Which remains.
Always.
As crystals in the eyes of the world
and memories in the gravest night.

ONCE A CATHOLIC

The Office for National Statistics data on religious views of Under 40's in South Lakeland shows:

2011   No religion 32%   Christianity 59%

2021   No religion 52%   Christianity 40%

A similar trend was seen across England and Wales.

2021 was the first time Christianity did not hold the top spot for an age group.

I can't recall just when I stopped believing. My mother was a Roman Catholic and each Sunday morning we walked by the canal to Mass. I think even then I had more interest in the canal. Maybe it was in my school days in a non-Catholic school, when I was excused morning assembly? I was sent for a Catholic top up to Father Birtles, who smelled of stale incense in a cassock encrusted with egg or snot. It could have been in the army in West Africa when I experienced a different ceremonial practice, which included tribal rituals and all night drumming. Later I witnessed smug, well endowed 'White Father' missionaries preaching resurrection. Another step was my Mum's funeral when, under a cracked crucifix, the priest ranted to a miniscule fandom of five regular ladies (all wearing green hats) that: *"Lucy Fox missed mass for many years."* and would therefore go to Hell and Damnation unless, by His Mercy, Jesus (or his Dad) took pity and gave Lucy a lift up to Eternity in the Glory of the Kingdom of God.

Certainly, by February 2023 at Billy's funeral in our old Parish Church in Ulverston, my (spiritually inclined) atheist position was confirmed. Age 59, Billy died suddenly of pneumonia. As a fruit and veg trader in our indoor market he was greatly respected. Hard working, always smiling, *"would help anyone"* and for 27 years a retained fireman with Cumbria Fire and Rescue Service. The Rector read to over 200 mourners an excellent eulogy written by the family. Unfortunately she then took off with the usual God script proselytizing that we are all sinners destined to endure our life on earth with the promise of Heaven where, if we repent, we will live happily ever after with our Redeemer.

"God made Billy," the Rector preached to his disabled mother in the front pew. Then from the Book of Ecclesiastes, Chapter Three, Verses 1-8. *"Dust and ashes have no dominion"* and *"There is a time to plant and a time to uproot"* (Veg man Billy would have liked that) but then, *"There is a time for love and a time for hate and a time for war and a time for peace."* I don't think so. Neither did other mourners. Billy a humble local man, led a good if short life. The town's people needed

to pay their respects to a valued colleague and for the majority, the church is currently the only method available. Maybe Billy was a believer or maybe his life (and death) were usurped and used for questionable dogma. The twenty Firefighters, as a dignified guard of honour outside, offered a more sincere and meaningful ceremony. Lined up each side of the church entrance, their yellow helmets placed carefully on the ground, with one on Billy's coffin, they gave the occasion dignity and respect. After the service their fire appliance led Billy's hearse through streets lined with mourners and then past the Market Hall for a final good bye. The Firefighters carried his coffin and they carried the day!

DEADLINES OR DEATHLINES

More than twenty people from our circle of friends and colleagues have died in recent memory. Some deaths were gentle, others hideous. All of them younger than we are.

Dignity in Dying www.dignityindying.org.uk is a campaign we support that works to make sure assisted dying law is safe, fair and compassionate. The Government's Health and Social Care Committee's Consultation on assisted dying is underway and is heading for its deadline in early 2023.

Our current law fails dying people and their loved ones, of whom research shows that 44% say they would break the law to help a loved one to die, thereby risking a 14 year jail sentence. Assisted dying for terminally ill, mentally competent adults is legal in Australia, New Zealand, Canada and 10 States in the US.

Now we are approaching our mid-eighties this is inevitably in our minds.

This is not about shortening life.

It is about shortening death.

HOME MADE LIFE

THE HOME MADE LIFE

In our garage a newly hatched swallow is learning to fly. It is scrabbling on the lip of a cardboard box, one of many containing old files. Twittering on telephone wires above, swallow parents search anxiously. It is a handy reminder of the recurring patterns and generational evolution of our own journey, as we lurched from one perch to another. A key part of our learning has been how to fuse the everyday with a heightened awareness.

Allowing the 'performative' to seep into our family life, striving for continuous creativity where aesthetic, radical and collective consciousness is the holistic norm; where a shift from the mundane to the extra-ordinary is partly a choice of perception and partly a matter of wilful luck.

July 2008 at The Beach House. We have the perfect opportunity to test our assertions. Stanley Greaves, an old friend and acclaimed artist from Guyana and Barbados, asks us to organise a betrothal ceremony for him and his new partner Leila. So at 5am, just before sunrise, I am under our wheelbarrow spraying WD 40 onto a squeaky wheel. Must not wake the neighbours! Four of us set off across the flat sands of the Bay with our wheelbarrow of ceremonial kit: ten small silk flags on garden sticks, laminated poems, a picnic hamper with fresh coffee, Bayjun Special Reserve Rum, warm croissants and accordion. Stanley was up late last night carving 'The Marking Stick' from a length of seasoned chestnut. He carries this and the rings, Leila brings fresh flowers while Sue helps me manoeuvre the unstable load.

Stanley and Leila stand west of The Rock facing the dawn sky and the turning tide. Using 'The Marking Stick' they draw in the sand a large heart with two adjacent diamonds while Sue and I install the flags in a semi circle behind them. As we wait for the sun to rise, a skein of geese honk past. After Sue sings Gibran's *Breaths* as a welcoming blessing and I read my betrothal poem, the couple step into the diamonds, left and right, to read two of Stanley's poems. Then, entering the heart together they exchange rings, make vows and sing *Drink to me only with thine eyes*. Finally they scatter petals in the lagoon round The Rock. We offer toasts with rum and coffee, I play *The Westmorland Waltz* on accordion and the couple dance, just as the sun emerges in full monty.

On the way back there is an uncanny surprise. On the vast empty beach we discover big paw prints. As we waited for sunrise all was quiet and any movement instantly discernible. Apart from the flock of geese nothing whatsoever crossed our path. Yet clearly **on top** of the broad tyre marks made by our wheel barrow, clear prints! A ghost wolf? Perception and luck again.

Back home we feast first on local eggs and bacon, later on barbecued chicken and French champagne.

Everyone makes decorations. Naomi a Japanese parasol laced with oystercatcher feathers, Reuben (7) a table centre tepee of bronze soldering rods stuck together with red insulating tape, holding green ferns and Rosa (5) a drawing of spidery lovers on parade. Round a brazier of oak logs we conjure up a cornucopia of music bouncing between English folk and Jamaican calypso. So, family, memories and cultures entwine in a shared and joyous affirmation with the home grown 'performative' well and truly embedded.

And the swallow? It flew away perfectly, of course.

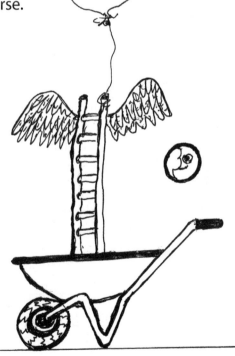

TWO NAMINGS

We were never hippies but, over 50 years ago, when we concocted a mid-summer naming ceremony for our son Daniel and other unsuspecting babies in Rosedale, a remote village on the North Yorkshire moors, chances are our neigbours thought we were.

A Chinese New Year story tells of a poor and hungry peasant who buys a statue of a beautiful girl. She comes to life. After celebrating with flowers and scarce food they live together and the woman bears a child. One day she is overcome with an inescapable longing to return to her statue self. So the man is left alone with the child.

In perfect sunshine 60 guests gather to sit on straw bales by a sheltered knoll resplendent with foxgloves and wild roses. After firecrackers, the slow twenty minute performance starts. A band with singers heralds in the peasant, in an oatmeal robe, white mask and big canvas sandals. Joined by a masked performer, portraying his statue, they become dreamlike puppets. At the end of the story the man, proud and protecting, holds his infant aloft. We then follow the musicians to the top of a small hill to find a bonfire, a flapping red banner and billowing pink smoke. On the cue of gongs, parents go forward holding their child(ren) high and calling their new names into the wind and the world. Followed by a traditional and comforting village spread of thin ham sandwiches, fat cream cakes and gallons of Yorkshire tea.

I remember the day well:

- All the babies (but sadly not all the parents) survive and thrive.
- We were given two rare and delicate Japanese fireworks which rocketed to the sky, exploding to release a paper toy soldier with a drum and blue paper elephant which parachuted slowly down to Rosedale.
- The big red banner was a mistake. Not only hippies but evidently Communists too!
- Another big mistake was our failure to brief Daniel's grandmother who, expecting a standard Christening, took a decade to forgive, or even mention, our pagan playacting.

2nd September 2001 Reuben our first grandchild, nearly a year old, is about to be named on a wide beach on the West shore of Morecambe Bay. For the ceremony his father, Duncan Copley, has constructed *Wishbone House*, an arched shelter made from two pairs of large oak wishbones and oak ribs mounted on a wooden raft and covered by an undulating willow wall. Parked overnight on the shoreline, on a precise East / West axis, our precious and fragile pavilion was slewed North / South into mud and reeds by a high tide, driven by an unexpected gale. So life (and blessings) shift!

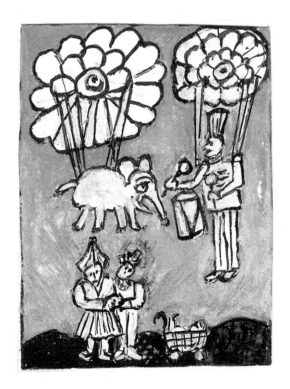

Families gather. Hannah, his mother, has prepared for us all small copper boats with sails. After writing wishes on the sails we float them on water in a large metal dish, sliced from the end of a disused shipyard boiler and enhanced with a blue silk sail embroidered with all Reuben's names. *Reuben Horatio Ashburner Fox Copley*. *Horatio* after my sea captain father (after Nelson) and *Ashburner* after his 86 year old great grandfather, who chuckles warmly nestling Reuben in his brawny arms.

Gilly Adams, the celebrant, calls us for speeches and toasts. Not too many. Soon it's over. Tears and farewells. Wishbone House to dismantle and another child happily set sail on another voyage!

A WELCOME BLESSING FOR REUBEN

Reuben,
welcome to the Bay
where sun shines and mists shimmer.
Here the sea sweeps in
to snatch the shingle.
Here storms rip ash and oak.
Minnows, shrimps and worms
settle and dart to eat each other,
while gannets and dunlins
and even pesky crows,
race to devour the cocktail of the tide.
A good place to be, where truth is clear
and beauty is certain but dangerous.

My father, great grandad to you, died in 1979.
A sailor who knew he could drown in the deep.
Your other great granddad is here today
a brick-man who knows how clay makes your
fingers raw.

Wherever you are tossed,
see what's true and know our cradle of love is here.
Be full of laughter and songs.
Play like crazy and never be afraid to weep.
Welcome, Reuben, welcome to this world.
May your voyage be wonderful and long.

CHANGING MY NAME

I am a late developer. It took me until my mid Forties before I realise I have never had a name of my own. I start as Susan Robinson, daughter of Mr and Mrs Robinson, then marry John Fox so in those days I automatically become Mrs Susan Fox. I have no ownership of these surnames, perfectly fine though they are. Nothing to do with me. They just came from my father and my husband.

I can have a name of my own choosing I realise, and I know straightaway what it will be. I have found my spot, my home and that place is The Gill. I will be Sue Gill. That feels right. I can own this name. I have lived here for several years with my family, never been made so welcome, and can find no reason to leave. Some older ladies in Ulverston still call me Mrs Fox and that is fine. I am still married to John Fox.

There was a prejudice amongst people of my generation around "the wife" being associated with a company or business that her husband led. She must only be there on sufferance. Despite the contribution she might be making, it carried a sense of apology.

Changing my name dissolved all that overnight. New people meet me in my own right and might later learn the family connections. Fearing to hurt my parents though and hating conflict, I left them believing that, because I work in the arts, it is a stage name.

My work in Rites of Passage sees me frequently working to devise secular ceremonies to mark milestones in people's lives. Should I as a middle aged woman not be having a Re-Naming Ceremony? I bottle out of inviting friends and colleagues to a self centred gathering. I leave it, I dither, but know that one day it has to happen.

The perfect occasion offers itself. In a community hall on The Gill. We have gathered with neighbours to say farewell to a lovely young couple who live here and are soon heading off. We've made the food, decorated the hall and played music together. There will never be a better opportunity, with family and immediate community from The Gill as witnesses. Without wishing to eclipse the party, I stand up and make an announcement. Unprepared. I say I am planning to change my name, and why it is significant for me. I want them to be the first to hear the news, and *"from today I would like to be known as Sue Gill."* Two grown men cry …

I make it all legal by Deed Poll and then set about the considerable admin notifying all the authorities.

Postscript: On the day of my 'lightbulb moment' something odd and significant occurred. It was a dull Sunday afternoon and I sat on the window seat on the top floor of our house, reading and reflecting. A car drove up and parked in front of the house, two well dressed strangers got out, a man and a woman. He had come to teach her water divining I soon realised. Taking a stick in each hand, he turned his back and walked slowly across the square, above where Gill Beck flows all year round, below the tarmac, as it heads out into the Bay.

He had taken only a few steps before both sticks vibrated strongly. As he continued walking in a straight line, they became still again. Turning to face her, he began to walk back and the pattern was repeated in the same area, exactly above Gill Beck. He handed her the sticks and her lessons began.

CAIRN

A cairn is a pile or stack of stones and rocks raised for a purpose - usually as a marker these days - whereas in the past they might also signify a burial mound.

Around areas with little vegetation - on the fellsides and mountainsides of the Lake District, the Andes or Mongolia - cairns mark routes to safety. They help people find their way where there may be few landmarks. Reaching a fork on an unfamiliar path, the walker can trust in the accumulated knowledge that has placed the next cairn in that precise spot. Cairns are guideposts for walkers and we have built them for thousands of years. Subject to weather and seasons, they could start to diminish unless repaired and re-stacked.

Unwritten lore is that a walker would never pass a cairn without adding a fresh stone, as a way of thanking those walkers ahead and looking out for the walker behind. A practical resource, a tool and a metaphor. Here elements speak at a deep level, reminding us of our shared humanity as we walk the landscape.

I was asked to lead a Ceremony of Remembrance for Great Ormond Street Hospital for Sick Children after the issue of unauthorised retention of children's organs came to light. They needed to apologise and make amends to the bereaved parents.

With the idea of creating a cairn at the venue on the day, we sent out an invitation to families to bring along a stone or a pebble from home. Hundreds of families travelled hundreds of miles to be there. The roll call of each and every name was read aloud from the stage with great dignity by one couple whose young son Jack had died, and who subsequently devoted their time to the hospital helpline for others going through the same loss. From the stage, we witnessed three hundred anxious strangers waiting to hear that one name. Their intake of breath, their grief was palpable, trembling up and down the rows, to and fro across the hall.

Stones, shells, some painted pebbles with names and messages all went onto the cairn during the afternoon. Families went through glass doors to a flagged court-yard open to the sky, where we had put some initial stones to start off the cairn. It was a magnet. Some made their offerings alone, others collectively. The cairn grew and acquired an identity. As it grew in detail, the mood lightened. Families felt they could choose their time to leave, knowing that something new and distinctive had been created by them all today.

It will remain there as a memorial to their children.

PAT-A-CAKE POLKA

DISMANTLING THE CIRCUS

Our first grandchildren, then aged about 10,
created a model of a circus as a Christmas gift
for us. Fashioned with willow sticks, wire, loops
of lights, sundry bits and pieces, and a Captain
Webb matchbox music box, it stayed by our bed
side until years later it fell apart. The collapse
came in 2020 when, in the big world outside, so
much else seemed to be breaking down as well.

For a while the whole edifice had been tottering.
Even faithful spiders wrapped their webs and left.
Carved bobbins on poles, evidently from
some mill or other, are not worth returning.

Trapeze acrobats shiny as copper wire
were coiled and poised for rigorous tumbling.
Strong men in leopard skins clambered for linen
bunting,
crocheted and remaindered from the last war.

A wire bicycle dreamt by Paul Klee, styled for athletic
fleas,
disappeared in uncalled for bedroom dust.
Outside the ring an irresistible cart horse,
with painted caravan, was clutched by infants
moons ago.
Batteries leak. Fairy lights bomb.
Last Saturday night the mirror ball went static.

One day it all gave way. No storm. No purpose. No audience.

Glue guns failed. Threads miscarried.
Sequins borne away by wind and wood lice.
Underneath the sea-salt deck though, as always,
Captain Webb remains; union-jacked and mu-
sic-boxed into our bones.

So one day the dot to dot, heel & toe pat-a-cake
polka of it all collapsed.
Just like that.

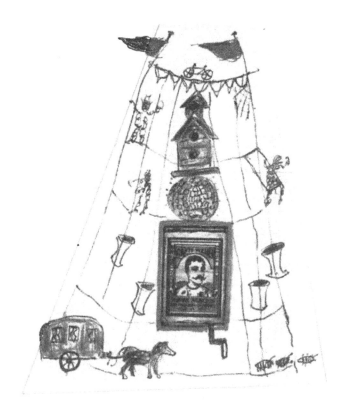

HANNAH

On Australia Day 26th January 2023 our daughter Hannah will have a fifty plus birthday. She has just finished activating Saturnalia – a dozen theatre events, outdoors in icy weather – to mark the 1900th anniversary of Hadrian's Wall. For a procession she created a key image, a canvas snail mounted on a slow moving tricycle, holding a projected animation of the planet Saturn, balefully unwinding within its spectral veils.

Twenty six years ago when the Fox family gathered in Capellades (Catalonia), in a brittle marble floored apartment, to make critical and difficult decisions about future work, she made another snail. An after dinner jewelled bread snail, laced with five blazing sparklers. A focussed playful interlude of welcome relief.

Hannah also made a special gift for me. Quietly she led me to the outside terrace where in the grey dusk she had carefully placed and illuminated a delicate procession of the tiniest glass animals you could imagine. Each a snowflake high. A crystal giraffe, an amber camel, two carmine ponies, a multi coloured cockerel and a golden hen. As if Chagall had miniaturised Noah's Ark. As if the night stars had fallen at my feet. As if ...

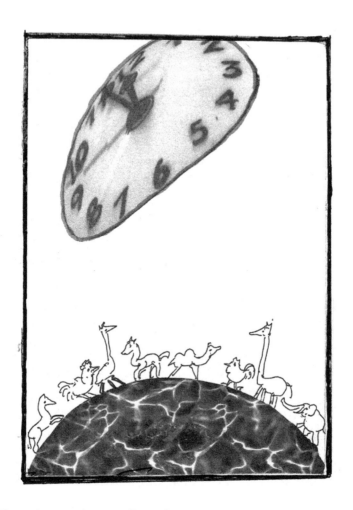

When Hannah was five she would see lights in the grass, that no one else could see and regularly found four leaf clovers.

When she was born the midwife said: "Here's one that has been here before."

I do sometimes wonder.

So many fabulous memories. And so much affection. Thank you lovely Hannah.

SWORDFISH

Luca our grandson, made this helicopter swordfish when he was six. He hammered and cut the metal, then found and assembled wire bag ties (used for sealing potato sacks) for the blades. A tiny piece of folded tin provides the stand. He is following his dad, our son Dan, who is an excellent inventor and hands on maker (who maybe gave him a bit of a hand?) and who, in turn, as a young boy, learned to hammer metal from Jamie, an artist blacksmith friend.

I wish someone had recorded what I did when I was six.

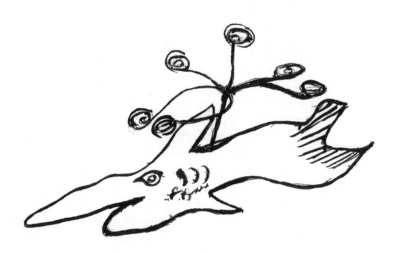

WORTH
WAITING FOR

FRIGILIANA

We had a wobble before I wrote this. In sentimental detail we revisit our 50th wedding anniversary (2012) in Rosaria, a rented villa in Frigiliana, Southern Spain. Who would be interested to read about a pair of seriously bonded heterosexual wrinklies, over proud of their two offspring and three grandchildren, reinforcing and celebrating their Marriage (an outmoded concept anyway) in an exotic retreat? With a rental of £1700 too when many can't afford houses, heat or food. ** Guilt.

Well, one aim of *eighty-something a lifelong conversation* is to recall examples from our life which reflect joys or sadnesses and pass on pleasures, insights or truths to hopefully strike chords with some readers. Some readers go on cruises. Some take two or three holidays each year. Some folk can't read and don't need to. A few stay warm in the library, while the majority have no spare time to give a toss anyway.

So here we are with indulgent quotes from my journal:

We are in a heritage converted mill, a mansion paradise of marble, wood and terracotta slabs with mountain views of ancient Andalucia, a shady terrace, cyprus

---

** We didn't want a huge party, just a close family gathering. So we paid for the villa and our hardworking family paid their own airfares and car hires.

trees and a curvaceous adobe pool. Enough space for our tribe of nine to dance and sing or be replete on barbecued squid, cuttlefish or chicken with unlimited Sangria, local Rioja and sunshine.

After dinner, infant bridesmaids in orange sarongs and an unlikely pageboy in green, scatter petals to lead us two to a top terrace under a near full moon. A trio of musicians with ukeleles sings *We're going to the Chapel*. We, the nervous couple, framed under a canopy of cream and purple paper streamers, glimpse a heart of red night lights cushioned on a millstone. Using long bamboos, a raft of candles is gently propelled across the pool. Gradually we gather near ancient earthenware pots (left over from Sinbad) and are invited to renew our vows.

The brandy did speak a little and the ink has smudged in the journal so all is not over clear but I believe I spoke of generations and invoked our long dead parents. I certainly proclaimed everlasting love for "*This woman Sue Gill*". Sue is not sure of her words either but she was delighted to have two granddaughter bridesmaids when in our original wedding 50 years before she refused to have any. *Some things are worth waiting for and seem to come round in the end*. This great ceremonial evening ended on more brandy and perilous acrobatics over the deep end, with a tumbling tableau of self-timed photos.

Perfect souvenirs. But where are they now? And where are Sparkle and Michael our two resident lizards?

THE CLARINET

In 1954 when I was 16 my first record was Chris Barber's band playing: *I scream, you scream. We all scream for ice cream*. Written in 1927 Ice-cream became a jazz standard. Chris Barber's arrangement was skilfully borrowed (conveniently in 1954) from a small New Orleans jazz combo featuring George Lewis. Lewis (1900-1968) a disabled ex docker, was one of the founding fathers of traditional jazz, an inventive improvising clarinet player. I wanted to play like him and I still try!

Clarinets then cost £16. To buy my own instrument I worked in a beer bottling factory humping crates on to wagons and, as a driver's mate, delivering them to Hull pubs. After two weeks of hard graft I had the cash. But on my last day an accident. Speedily barrowing metal crates on a two wheel trolly I hit an upturned paving stone. The top crate bounced up into my mouth smashing the two front teeth needed to play a clarinet. Unfortunately the allotted dentist was distracted and clumsy - his wife had just killed herself - so treatment was intermittent and for some time my teeth were wonky.

Before I was 18 I was called up for National Service and took my 'ebony stick' with me on my posting to Ghana. One of my (few) regrets is that I didn't apply from the start to be trained in a military band instead of becoming a fledgling second lieutenant in West Africa, where I was responsible for 30 soldiers and their extensive families. I did try to practice the clarinet, but out of tune improvisations are not encouraged by the officer class. Dissuasion came with thunder flashes lobbed into my flimsy living quarters rocking down dust and rats from the fragile ceiling. I had to give up!

Over 60 years later though I am nearly there. My clarinet has morphed into a soprano saxophone (courtesy of Sidney Bechet) but George Lewis, is still my mentor. I know I am nearly there because after playing for 20 years in Blast Furness, a street band, last week in rehearsal I improvised another wild solo.

"Best yet," they said.

Never too late!

STUMBLING ACROSS STANLEY

Visiting the new Hepworth Gallery in Wakefield I head for Stanley Spencer's paintings, which I love. Looking into a glass topped cabinet I read a page in one of his notebooks and scribble down what he had written.

'I suddenly became aware that life was a wonderful affair; a great event happening everyday; the chief events being morning, afternoon, evening.
My first desire was to celebrate and solemnise these events …. Taking solid chunks of my own life and put-ting it on canvas.
I like my life so much that I would cover every empty space on a wall with it.
Painting pictures is my way of giving praise;
I don't know to whom, it doesn't stop me from giving.'

These few sentences stop me in my tracks. I resonate entirely with Stanley.

I love my life. I would like to cover every sheet of paper with it.

Writing is my way of giving praise; I don't know to whom either but that doesn't stop me from giving.

Thank you Stanley.

MILE WIDE & INCH DEEP

Looking back to the early years of my working life with Welfare State International I would describe my skill base as one mile wide, one inch deep. I was adequate at lots of things: singing, project management, delivering lectures and workshops, cooking feasts, street performing, HGV truck driving.

My current work into Rites of Passage, creating new ceremonies and celebrations, feels very different. I might venture to describe my practice now as: approaching one mile deep and one inch wide.
At long last I have found the work that uses all of me.

GARMENT

I have been wearing this garment next to my skin
for as long as I can remember.

It is soft. And light. Made from the finest thread.
It fits perfectly across bony shoulders and down my
long arms to the wrists.
It moves as I move. No jarring.
I hardly know it's there.

This garment is my life.

I think about unravelling it,
carefully unstitching row by row by row.
Only this way might I figure out
just how much it all amounts to,
just how I've got to be this old.

Uncoiling the stitches, reeling out the rows,
I wind the thread into a ball.
Not too slack, not too tight.
In the palms of my hands
time grows plump and full.

Half way back, that knot
where things came apart for a while.
The repair has held.

This thread is the cat's cradle of my world.

I couldn't do this next bit by myself.
I need a second pair of hands.
The agile fingers of a granddaughter.

Heads close together and we begin.
I hold the thread in precise rigging between my left
and right.
She duets her little fingers, first hooking and lifting,
then crossing
to reveal the first map, the horizontal.
Turn by turn we would pass diagrams of wisdom
exchange new geometries, breathing through
generations.
She must choose her moment and teach our next
two girls.

I think about unravelling it, but I don't, I change my
mind.
I think about stock taking my life, but I don't, I
change my mind.
I think about thinking about it, but I don't.
I keep on wearing it next to my skin.

50 CLOVES OF
GARLIC

RABBITS

I swot flies. I trap mice and rats. I once drowned some unwanted kittens. I visited a slaughter house and had nightmares. I eat meat. I don't like killing animals, or the thought of killing them, but I am not a vegetarian.

So to rabbits. A few years ago there were big rabbits nibbling on the beach below our house. Now there are none. Likely they have been killed by disease maybe deliberately.

Statistics tell us there are over 30 million wild rabbits in the UK. Potentially a lot of home grown meat. To kill them you can shoot, trap or cage them (and then break their necks. *"It's a knack."*) I prefer a sharp axe on a wood block.

There was a time, before we bought them oven ready from supermarkets, that I followed this procedure: Once killed, cut off the legs and the head. Skin them (like peeling a banana). Gut them fast as the stomach is full of cellulose and bacteria. Squeeze the bladder before the urine taints the flesh. Finish gutting. Open up the cavity at the back. Remove the small gall bladder lump, which renders the liver bitter. Remove any blood. Put the carcass in the fridge and paunch overnight in salted water.[***] Then cook.

[***] BBC Radio 4 Food Programme 6/10/08. interview with Mark Gilchrist owner and head chef of the catering company 'Game for Everything'

There is an inspirational and delicious recipe for braised rabbit in *The Artist's Table* published by the Bishop Suter Gallery in New Zealand. A favourite of Jens Hansen (the jeweller commissioned to make the 'One Ring' for the *Lord of the Rings* movie trilogy). He used two jointed rabbits, 50 cloves of unpeeled garlic, 24 shallots, 124g of smoked streaky bacon, half a bottle of white wine, a *good slurp of sherry*, a pint of chicken stock, 6 bay leaves, 3 tablespoons of dijon mustard, thyme, salt, pepper and olive oil. Cooked for 1 hour at 150 C.

Pick five hungry friends, a reasonable red wine, crusty bread and feast. Rabbit rabbit.

RAT

There's a rat in the kitchen.
A very intelligent rat.
Leaps to snap the strings
of a suspended bag of grain.
Gnaws floor boards one inch thick.
It gnaws at night
scratching and clawing.
Wakes us up.
Throw a boot over the landing.
Flood the floor with light.
Tread carefully downstairs.
Will it run over my toes?
There it goes, a scruffy handbag
vanishing in the gap by the sink.

Prime the trap with kipper bits.
Lay a trail with eggshells camouflaged.
Then wait. Wait for the click.
Two days and nights. More gnawing.
Click! The trap is sprung.
Yet no rat impaled.
Clever rat.

Under the cooker though
a tail protrudes.
Long, rubbery and strong.
Is it dead?

Pinch the tail with kitchen paper,
pull it slowly into sight.
The stiff corpse of an old creature.
We broke its back.

Grey fur, matted yet soft
as moss in a Moses basket.
Wire scar across the thigh
and the last black droppings
of a frightened clever rat.

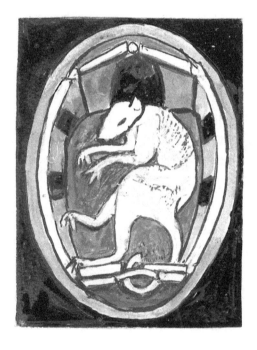

The drawing illustrates a mummified rat in a derelict ark.
When Reuben our grandson was six he found a plastic toy ark
washed up on the beach. Later the desiccated rat turned up
under some floor boards and somehow its carcass ended up
lying peacefully inside the ark, with a mysterious poignancy.

DISHWASHER

It took me 40 years before I got a dishwasher. I had always despised them as affluent first world luxury, unsustainable capitalist decadence. I could run a household without such indulgence.

I live my life one day at a time. Today completed, tomorrow start again with a clean slate. This has developed from being a cook - frequently in the past cooking for numbers of artists and participants in our events.

Now, domestic days take on a symphonic structure:

1st movement - **OVERTURE** - brisk and lively. Planning the menu, finding contrasting courses, complementary flavours, assembling ingredients and starting the preparation.

2nd movement - **ANDANTE** - slower, concentrated, carefully timed cooking. Progressions - major to minor - and back again. Overall balance of colour, texture, taste.

3rd movement - **MINUET** - energetic. Serving it up, keeping in mind harmonic accompaniments over the bass line, however simple.

4th movement - **FINALE** - rollicking, feasting. Finish. Empty plates. Job's a good'un.

"But what a shame after all that work and there's nothing left," is a familiar response from visitors. I would see it as a failure if there was anything left.

But I need to add another movement here to my symphony:

5th movement - **CODA** - clear up, clean up. Digestion. Reflection.

I am comfortable with this rhythm. A 24 hour cycle is something I can grasp and keep in focus. The installation of the dishwasher brought this unexpected coda to the classical structure of my day.

At the Beach House, John and I cook our evening meal from scratch - never together! - searching out particular and sometimes quite lavish recipes - the sort that call for several pots and pans. We often end up eating fairly late so the accumulated washing up would get left - smeary and encrusted - and squander a brand new morning. Often done in a rush with tacky results.

Yet the dishwasher, loaded at night, delivers up sparkling crockery, cutlery and glasses, fit to use, fit to offer to visitors. In the blink of an eye the dishwasher can be emptied.

A **PRELUDE** to tomorrow, whatever that might bring.

DEAD GOOD
BREAD RECIPE
perfect for sculptural bread that's still good to eat.

Ingredients

600g strong bread flour - say 500g wholemeal / 100g strong white, 1 dessertspoon salt, 1 dessert-spoon soft brown sugar or honey, 1 good 'glug' of olive oil, 1 sachet dried yeast, 350m warm water with 1 desstsp black treacle dissolved in it. Herbs and spices to choose from: rosemary, sage, cumin seeds, sliced pitted olives, walnuts, chopped sun-dried tomatoes, chopped garlic, onion.

Method

Mix all dry ingredients together in a basin:

dried yeast, flour, salt, herbs or spices, sugar or honey then pour in the oil.

Make a hole in dry ingredients, add warm water and knead for 10 minutes on a lightly floured surface, until the dough becomes smooth and shiny. Lightly grease a clean bowl with some oil. Put the dough back into the bowl and cover with cling film. Leave to rise in a warm place until it doubles in size.1-2 hours. Put it into greased loaf tin. To make rolls, roll it gently 3-5cm thickness with a rolling pin, then with a sharp knife, cut the dough into 12-15 pieces, shape them with your hands and space them on a greased baking tray. Brush the dough with milk. It will brown as it cooks.

To make a plait, roll dough gently into a narrow rectangle approx 30 x 15cm. Make two longways parallel cuts with a sharp knife, making sure you stop cutting about 3cm before the end, so the strips are still joined. Gently lift one strip left over right, other strip right over left, and again and again to make your plait. Work fast. Brush with milk, secure the ends of your strips, lift onto a greased baking tray.

OR: Have fun shaping the whole dough to make a fish, the sun, an animal, a person, a star ... Keep it chunky. [The bits you cut off you can bake as small rolls]. Use anything from your kitchen drawer to add texture to your image by pressing, snipping, cutting the dough boldly. Brush with milk, get it into the oven fast!

Gas Mark 8, Hot Air 200. Middle shelf. Rolls 15 mins, loaves 30-35 mins. To check if the loaf is cooked, remove it from its tin, turn it upside down and knock on the bottom. If it sounds hollow it is done, if not, replace it in the tin upside down. Cook a few minutes more. When ready, rub the top with butter while still warm to give an impressive shiny surface.

SCULPTURAL BREAD

By quadrupling these quantities you would have enough dough to make two sculptural bread plaques to present at an event. The dough models well but will continue to rise as you design your image. Work fast, get it into the oven as fast as possible. Offcuts of dough can be shaped and baked as rolls.

WEDDING BREAD: usually baked with symbolic decoration in the bride's home, it is an integral part of the ceremony in Crete and the Ukraine. Decorative holiday bread is still common in many European countries — particularly at Christmas and Easter. An Italian fertility bread shows a three-breasted woman. Welfare State has helped to arrange 3 marriages, and we used the following recipe for the bread:

6lb. brown wholemeal flour
2 tblsp. brown sugar
2 tblsp. black treacle
salt to taste: try 1 dsstsp.

4 oz. vegetable fat
6 oz. fresh yeast
2½ pts. warm water.

Use sponge method. This gives enough for 2 large plaques + plenty to spare for some rolls.

Work fast! The dough models well, but it is live a will continue to rise until in the oven. At one wedding the bride's mother was aghast at the sight of the bride's breasts swelling visibly in the kitchen.

KITH & KIN

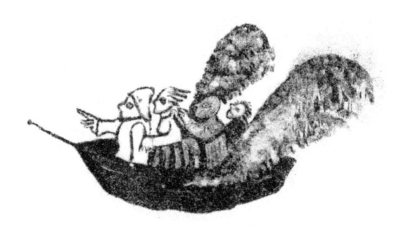

THE VOYAGE

Lyrics Johnny Duhan / Sung by Christy Moore

I am a sailor, you're my first mate We signed on
together, we coupled our fate Hauled up our anchor,
determined not to fail For the hearts treasure,
together we set sail

With no maps to guide us we steered our own
course Rode out the storms when the winds were
gale force Sat out the doldrums in patience and
hope Working together we learned how to cope

*Life is an ocean and love is a boat In troubled waters
that keeps us afloat When we started the voyage, there
was just me and you Now gathered round us,
we have our own crew*

Together we're sailing this ship We built it with care
to last the whole trip Our true destination's not
marked on any charts We're navigating to the shores
of the heart

*Life is an ocean and love is a boat In troubled waters
that keeps us afloat When we started the voyage, there
was just me and you Now gathered round us,
we have our own crew.*

This song captures the story of our lives. I emailed Johnny Duhan to ask his permission to include these lyrics in our book *eighty-something a lifetime of conversation* unsure of whether I would hear from him. Within a few hours he sent a reply:

'*What a lovely surprise to brighten up a dull day here in the west of Ireland, where my first mate and I [both in our early 70's] are still steering the ship of our dreams, with support of our crew, who are in fact due to visit us tonight for a birthday party for their mother.*

Of course you have my full approval to print the lyrics of The Voyage in your book and I wish you the best of luck with it ....'

NATIVITY

Our five grandchildren, now aged between 22 and 9, were all educated at the same C of E village primary school with only 60 children on the roll. As a dutiful grandad I have attended a large number of Nativity Plays. It is a good school but, uneasy with the theology (and its perpetuation), I keep my blood pressure down by sketching in my notebook during the performances.

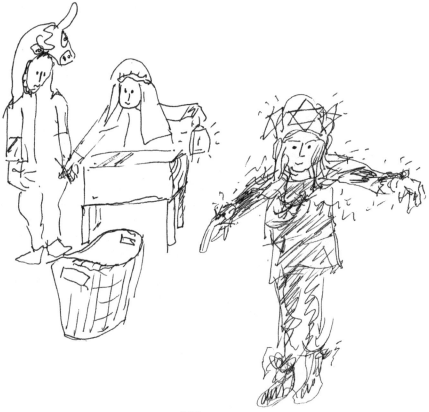

The Christian story goes that we are all sinners and through God sacrificing his only son (born of a virgin) we are offered redemption, forgiveness and ever lasting life in Heaven. This simplistic fable has, unbelievably, inspired centuries of stunning art and centuries of oppression too. Belief is now falling and Christianity is probably outmoded.

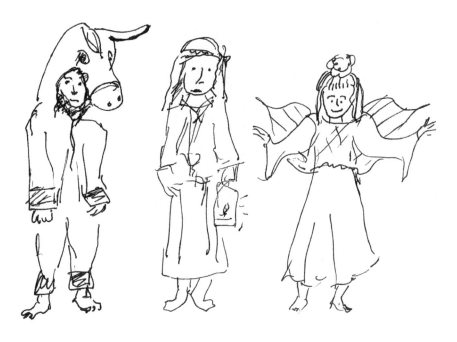

So for the 'time being' I am an atheist searching for a new ecological system, to hold and comfort us; a framework free of hierarchy, fear and proselytizers, where perspective and understanding encompass both lament and celebration.

SISTER & BROTHER BIRTHDAY

Twin grandchildren turn 8. Nana takes them on a day out. A day long game, with surprises, maybe the odd challenge, certainly a bit of mayhem and fun.

Get on a train at Ulverston station heading south. Count 8 rows of seats from the door and sit down.

This journey will take 16 minutes - two times 8. Disembark to explore Barrow in Furness.

Outside the glass front doors of the Law Courts dare to do 8 cartwheels on the forecourt or 8 forward rolls over the rail before security gets anxious.

Into the Children's Library. The massive room is totally re-modelled with the installation of a large 'boat' to climb up into and find a den space to stowaway. Tackle the Quiz. Quite tricky if not difficult until we spot clues and answers sneakily pinned up under shelves, above doors, round corners … All answers correct. Certificates!!

Lunch time. There's a nearby cafe, find a table, sit down and order the 8th item on the menu. Fortunately it's pizza.

Shopping. Head for the large charity shop. £8 each to spend on an outfit. Luca spots a red and black hoodie he likes in his size, that says PLAYSTATION on the front. Sorted. Bel finds the clothes boring, so chooses four books and a cuddly animal and has change to spare.

Detectives next: how many restaurants can we see with foreign names? Wai Ming, Izgara, Marmaris, Baan Siam, Dodona, Mithali, Kapadokya, Dhaba …..

Back on the train, then off to the Beach House for a fire down on the shore. 8 matches only to light it.

Teatime up in the house. Pasta with tuna and mayo, baby sweetcorns, little chipolatas, cubes of pineapple, slices of cucumber ……. Are we still counting to 8?

Sleepover. In bed by 8? NO CHANCE.

8 pancakes to mix and toss in the morning while we are still in pyjamas.
Sugar and lemon? Who's for Maple syrup?

BLOSSOMS FOR BEL

Each year for five days in April
(give or take a gale)
our cherry blossom tugs away.

Eight years ago to the day,
Baby Bel, two weeks old, is in my arms,
sucking my oily painting sweater.
Blissed out and rocking with
flamenco petals, snatched
on a gentle breeze.

Blossoms go.
Cherries come.
Blackbirds gorge.
Another year gone.

Now you are eight Bel,
and in your cartwheel days,
you paint angels with strawberry wings,
cuddle bears with raspberry ears
and sleep with dragon girls.

Will you count each blossom time and
sample the years that tug away?
Will you age to gather the amazements
of a life time's cache of petals?

Will you, lovely Bel?

BIRTHDAY LETTER TO ONE OF MY GRANDDAUGHTERS
The Beach House, Friday 5th March 2021

Dear Granddaughter,

You are now 18 and I am 82. We have an 8 in common. Over 60 years between us but I hope not quite worlds apart. For me at 18 I was conscripted to do National Service in Ghana. A long way away and no IT then. So I hand wrote letters to Sue (your Nana). Some of her replies are still waiting, hidden in a trunk in my studio. Nana was about 17 then. She once revealed she made a party dress out of all my letters and danced them through a celebratory fire on a wild moor. Excess is a handy default position.

18 is for dancing. Excessively and supremely ….. as you do. When you reach the heights, as you will, I will be there in body or spirit or both. Doubtless armed with electronic paraphernalia but also with pen and notebook too. Drawing for my pleasure and to laud to the world your style and energy and fabulous youthful being.

60 years ago in Africa I survived English Officer snobbery by playing football with my platoon of stroppy black soldiers. I was centre forward. A key position. I am

sure, despite the convolutions of institutions, you will thrive in a key position too. And you will shine while continuing to dance your heart out. I will be about. Not quite in football shorts, but in full kit of pride, joy and love for you. Happy 18th!

Grandad John, (With help from Sue, Nana Beach House). XX

Thursday 16th February 2023

My granddaughter now twenty and in her second year of professional training in Contemporary Dance just sent us a video of her latest student work. Based on my *Lullaby* poem and lasting three minutes, in her words her solo is *"About generations, love and mothering, sadness and loss, ageing and change".* It is a moving and profound work. In a collaborative process she recorded two voices: a child (her cousin) and an old woman (her grandmother) each speaking the words and fused these with a score created by musician friends. She describes herself as *"Mothering the child she once was."*

I am writing about it here, not just because I am proud of my granddaughter and am flattered she used my poem, but because in a book designed to share lessons and experiences, her journey demonstrates so much of what we hope for. As a child she walked with her grandmother, at low tide, on the beautiful and dangerous sands of Morecambe Bay. As a teenager in lockdown she came here to dance. Now her dance reveals she has absorbed the power of the seascape, understands the nature and progress of generations and has worked tirelessly and skilfully to articulate her feelings and concerns via her chosen art form. She already under-stands what an artist has to do. My belief is that we all have such potential and my hope, my wish is that every young person gains, as a right, access to this process of creative growing.

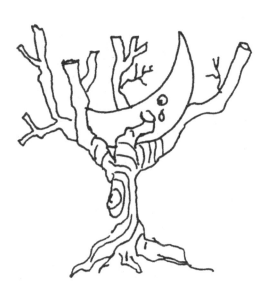

LULLABY

The score for this song/poem, composed by the
late Tim Fleming, is printed in Foxy's Song Book.

Hush now baby,
hush now baby hush.
Tide going out
tide going out.

No reflections tonight,
no stars in the sand, tide going out.
The world's not upside down.
Follow the plough to the pole star
held forever still.

Hush now baby hush.
The world's not upside down
The world's not upside down.
Lie you down, lie you down and sleep away,
close your eyes, close your eyes and leave the day.
May you dream of stars above the Bay.

The world's not upside down.
Follow the plough, to the pole star
held forever still.

TWELVE OF US
Christmas Dinner 2022

Sue, John, Hannah, Dan, Naomi, Reuben, Rosa, Rowan, Luca, Bel, Tony, Alastair.

Thank you all for coming.

Thanks to Hannah and Rosa for organising table and lighting. Sue for the food, and Jenny Wilson for the wine. It is a long time since we had twelve people round this table.

Twelve is a good number. A full football team with one reserve. Also Jesus had twelve close mates and it's his birthday today. So it can't be bad. Adding the number of years us twelve have been around comes to 449.

On both the public and private front it has not been an easy year. Some of you have suffered considerable stress. So we hope that this small gathering can be a peaceful, joyous and special family treat. So good you have come to be with Sue and I at the Beach House. Thank you so much. A 16th century nursery rime reads:

Christmas comes but once a year
and when it comes it brings good cheer.
But when it's gone it's never near.

Things do come and go. Are here and disappear. Are wonderful and sad and wonderful again. I was pleased to discover when I put up the Christmas lights that the sturdy nails from last year were still there. So something remains.

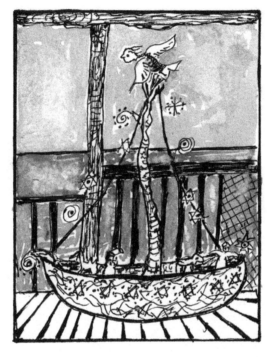

There is often a dark angel. But believe me the one at the top of the mast on our Christmas boat, put there by Bel and Luca, glows golden in moonlight.

And there is a curlew. I once wrote a poem asking what you would give for the last call of the last curlew? Well there is one in the Bay. We hear its melancholy call every day.

So here is a positive toast. Cheers to a joyous and creative 2023.

CODA

LAST FERRY

The ferryman has always been the mythic character who takes us across the water at the end of life to the other side, to who knows what? or where?

Canadian poet Don McKay wrote a tantalisingly shrewd poem *Taking the Ferry*.

Several Canadians we know live on small islands in the lakes and lagoons in Ontario and British Columbia and each morning take the ferry to their office in the city. He writes about the drudgery of this way of life until it is time to take the last ferry.

He lines up at the terminal with other weary souls to step on board for this journey.

Looking up as the skipper steps out onto the bridge, he exclaims:

"So it was you, all along buddy… The one I never recognised but somehow knew.
I should have known …" as he laboriously steps aboard.

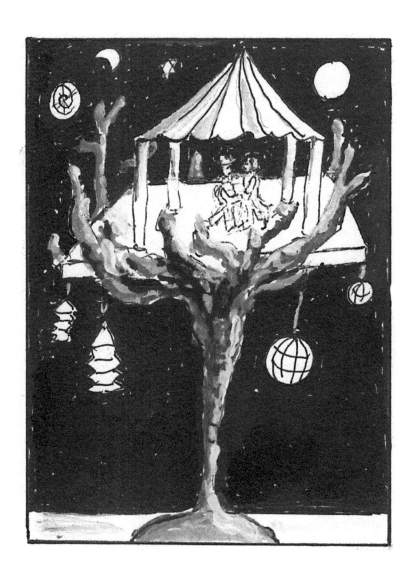

WHO WROTE WHAT?

JOHN FOX

Stick in the Mind, Skeleton, Mutton Birds, MBE, Cancer, One Time Rock, Mr Punch, Alone, Invocation for Tim, Once, Once a Catholic, The Home Made Life, Two Namings, Reuben Welcome Blessing, Dismantling the Circus, Hannah, Swordfish, Frigiliana, Clarinet, Rabbits, Rat, Nativity, Blossoms for Bel, Letter to my Granddaughter, Twelve of Us.

SUE GILL

Morning House, Frame Raising, Touch, Sanctuary, Head Hands Heart, Letter to my Mum, First Time, Handfuls of Clay, Bone Deep, Hospital Vocabulary, The Rock, Sea Washed Glass, Wave from the Ocean, The Bellwoman, One for Sorrow, Deadlines and Deathlines, Changing my Name, Cairn, Stumbling across Stanley, Mile Wide Inch Deep, Garment, Dishwasher, Bread Recipe, The Voyage, Sister Brother Birthday, Last Ferry.

THANKS to Gilly Adams for proof-reading.

BIOGRAPHIES

We have lived, worked and played together for a very long time. Our main vehicle has been directing the legendary Welfare State International (WSI) 1968-2006 which achieved an international reputation for pioneering site specific theatre, fire-shows, installations, lantern parades and secular ceremonies for Rites of Passage. In 2006 we archived WSI to start Dead Good Guides (DGG) which continues to train celebrants, create occasional sculpture trails and events and give keynote provocations and invigorating workshops.

www.deadgoodguides.co.uk
www.welfare-state.org

PUBLICATIONS

Engineers of the Imagination: Methuen. (WSI Handbook) Coult and Kershaw. 1983/90.

Matey Boy: Iron Press. Epic poem Kevin Fegan, linoprints John Fox. 1991.

The Dead Good Funerals Book: Sue Gill, John Fox. 1996/2004.

Ground: John Fox. Poems, woodcuts and linocuts. Ed. Gilly Adams. 1998.

The Dead Good Time Capsule Book: John Fox. Ed. Gill Gill. 1999.

Dead Good Book of Namings & Baby Welcoming Ceremonies: ed. J.How, Sue Gill, John Fox. 1999.

You Never Know John Fox. Poems. 2011-2022.

Eyes on Stalks: Methuen. John Fox. Personal account of WSI with drawings. 2002.

The Rain Days: John Fox. Poems. 2021.

Foxy's Song Book: Fifty one songs. Lyrics John Fox, music scores by seven composers. 2021.

In All My Born Days: Sue Gill. Biographical essays. 2022.

Please purchase our books via PayPal from: www.deadgoodguides.co.uk

Rites of Passage

Dead Good Guides, with Sue Gill and Gilly Adams, offer two four day courses every year on the nuts and bolts of personal and secular ceremonies for Rites of Passage. For further information: www.deadgoodguides.co.uk

Ingram Content Group UK Ltd.
Milton Keynes UK
UKHW041813260323
419133UK00004B/84/J